Enlarge My Coast

Enlarge My Coast

My India Song

BARRY BLACKSTONE

RESOURCE *Publications* · Eugene, Oregon

ENLARGE MY COAST
My India Song

Copyright © 2013 Barry Blackstone. All rights reserved. Except for brief quotations in critical publications or reviews, no part of this book may be reproduced in any manner without prior written permission from the publisher. Write: Permissions, Wipf and Stock Publishers, 199 W. 8th Ave., Suite 3, Eugene, OR 97401.

Wipf & Stock
An Imprint of Wipf and Stock Publishers
199 W. 8th Ave., Suite 3
Eugene, OR 97401
www.wipfandstock.com

ISBN 13: 978-1-62032-881-1
Manufactured in the U.S.A.

All Scripture quotations are taken from the Holy Bible, Authorized (King James) Version.

I dedicate this book to the members of the Emmanuel Baptist Church of Ellsworth, Maine which were responsible for me going to India for a third time. Their gracious giving, spectacular support, and generous gift will remain a testimony to the people of Kerala for years to come. I also thank Russ Coffin for joining me on this Indian adventure; our shared experiences will forever be remembered!

Contents

Prelude: My India Song / ix

1. Where in the World Is Marnie? / 1
2. Asking an Indian Question to an American Pastor / 3
3. A Bug in the Grout / 5
4. Unexpected Stay in Trivandrum / 7
5. Russ's Amazing Race / 9
6. A Caribbean Marnie / 11
7. John's Funeral / 13
8. A Scooter for Pastor Paul / 16
9. Old Messages and Old Friends / 17
10. Handing Out Awards at Bethany School / 19
11. Three Days of Sermons / 21
12. The Regions Beyond / 23
13. Cooking Pancakes over an Open Fire / 25
14. A Bell for KBBC / 27
15. The Old Paths-Graduation Day / 29
16. Saturday Blessings / 31
17. It Was Made of Bricks / 33
18. This House of God / 35
19. The First Parsonage / 37
20. Indian Houseboat Ride / 39
21. A Four-Hour Tour / 41
22. Goodbye to Russ / 43

Contents

23 A Kerala Chorus Book / 45
24 A Dry, Thirsty Land / 48
25 Triple B on Elephant Hill / 50
26 Lost in the Mountains of Kerala / 52
27 Rabbit for Lunch / 53
28 The Two Jewels of India / 56
29 A Birthday in a Foreign Land / 58
30 Fifty-Eight Colony / 61
31 The Four Musketeers / 64
32 A Train Ride in India / 66
33 Train Log / 68
34 Good Morning Andrah Pardesh! / 70
35 Guntakel Baptist Church / 72
36 The Journey to Kanekkallu / 74
37 Ellie of Kanekel / 76
38 Cell Phone Towers and Hindu Temples / 78
39 Harvest Time in Andrah Pardesh / 80
40 Street People of Kanekel / 82
41 A Private Chef / 84
42 Last Bus from Rayadurg / 86
43 The Boys of Orissa / 88
44 Tears under the Trees / 90
45 Bullock Cart Driver for Christ / 93
46 Other Jobs, but One Passion! / 95
47 Just the Ordinary / 97
48 Youth Rally at Kanekel / 99
49 Portrait of the Persecuted / 101
50 David, Rupert, and John Kennedy / 103
51 Ordination Sunday / 105

Contents

52   And Then There Were Three / 107
53   Police Raid at Four in the Morning! / 109
54   Second-class on an Indian Train / 111
55   Indian Beggars / 113
56   Hour by Hour / 115
57   Rendezvous at Kalpadi / 117
58   Picking Rice out of the Dirt / 119
59   Night Train to Kochi / 121
60   Saying Goodbye to Anna / 123
61   Strawberry Ice Cream / 125
62   Last Day in Edayappara / 127
63   Reviewing the Trip / 129
64   Blessings and More Blessings / 131
65   Daily Record / 133

   Postlude: Returning to my Coast   137

Prelude

My India Song

TO SAY THAT I have fallen in love with the land of India would be an understatement at best. Don't get me wrong, I am a Maineaic through and through and I still believe that the United States is the greatest country in the world, and certainly remains the best country in the world to live in. But there is something about India that has gotten into my heart and settled in my soul. Perhaps, this poem I wrote one stormy night after a mid-week prayer service at a rural Kerala church will highlight and underline this growing affection. I simply call it 'My India Song': (it also can be sung to W. G. Cooper's music for W. D. Cornell's classic church hymn, 'Wonderful Peace')

Far away in the vastness of India tonight,
Echoes the thunder and lighting of rain.
In flashes of glory it unceasingly rolls,
Every crash in a celestial strain.

What a treasure I have in this wonderful place,
Buried deep in the Kerala hills.
For the joy it bestows, and the friendship that grows,
Every day is a blessing that thrills.

I am resting tonight in this heavenly spot,
Resting calmly in my Saviour's good graces.
For I'm kept from all dangers, all harm, and alarm,
By a wonderful group of brown faces.

Prelude

When I think of my home in the Heaven's of light,
And I dream of the ending of time.
For me, it will be as an Indian sunrise,
Christ's coming will be so sublime.

Chorus:
Joy, joy, marvelous joy, falling down
From God's throne in the sky.
Filling my spirit, forever, always,
In a breathless and spectacular high!

Come with me for a third time into the subcontinent of Asia. Travel with me again to the tropical State of Kerala as I fulfill a four-year dream in seeing a sanctuary and parsonage built for the dear believers of the Venmony Baptist Church. I will be journeying this time with a dear friend and church deacon, Russ Coffin. It was through the gracious giving of the members of the Emmanuel Baptist Church this India project was completed. Despite their own building needs, the people of Emmanuel practiced the Lord's great admonition:

It is more blessed to give than receive! (Acts 20:35)

Also I was able to share the wonders and wants of India through the eyes of another person (Russ Coffin). Enjoy with us the fascination of watching a working elephant beside a rural road; the attempts of catching on film five people on a motorcycle at one time; a houseboat ride on Kerala's largest lake; listening to Russ's first sermon; graduation day at Kerala Baptist Bible College; an Indian barbeque of pancakes and omelets, and a journey on the infamous Indian railway into the backcountry of central India. As in my other India books, "Though None Go With Me" and "Though One Go With Me", share the practical, spiritual lessons I learned on this trip to India and my first mission's trip to the State of Andrah Pardesh as the guest evangelist for the Independent Gospel Baptist Churches and Associated Missions of India. Because I stayed two weeks longer than Russ, share in the personal experience of driving a bullock cart, eating an Indian catfish, preaching in a thatched-roof church, being surprised by a police raid at four in the morning, and witnessing more people coming to Christ at one time than any

Prelude

other time in my ministry. Journey with me for a month into the unpredictable land of India and enjoy the surprises around each corner; the fellowship will be sweet and the friendships made will be eternal!

I never remembered praying Jabez's famous prayer of I Chronicles 4:10, but I can see with each trip to India that the Good Lord in His wise providence has "enlarged my coast." From the coast of Maine to the coast of Kerala, I now have a broader vision, a deeper understanding, and a larger field of service than I have ever had before. Once again on this trip I will explore corners of God's wide harvest field that I never imagined I would and find that as God has 'enlarged my coast' He has also 'enlarged my heart' (Psalms 119:32) for the people of India and 'enlarged my steps' (Psalms 18:36) in the place called India!

Barry Blackstone

1

Where in the World Is Marnie?

Russ Coffin and I left our home state of Maine on the afternoon of February 17, 2010 (interestingly, the 30th birthday of my last traveling companion to India, my daughter Marnie), and flew from Bangor to New York City. There we had a seven hour layover before boarding our Qatar Air flight to Doha, Qatar, 6697 miles away! That flight took us across the Atlantic Ocean, through the gates of Gibraltar into the Mediterranean Sea, down through Egypt and the Red Sea before crossing Saudi Arabia landing in Doha eleven hours and forty-five minutes later. It was February 18th before we finally boarded another Qatar flight to Trivandrum, India, 2037 miles across the Arabian Sea, a flight of another six hours. It was February 19th when we finally landed safely on the coast of Kerala exactly 32 hours after we left our homes on the coast of Maine, and there to greet us were my two dear friends from previous trips: Binu and Shaju!

Because we landed at 4 AM and the 'boys' had been at the airport at 3 AM, our first stop was at the MoonStar Motel for a shower and a nap. It was here Russ experienced for the first time the downside of India. Despite the sun not being up yet, the humidity and heat were already oppressive (we would see temperatures reach 124 before we left), and then there was the motel. I had stayed at this very same motel on at least three occasions, but I had not been there since 2007. In that period of time the owners had let the place go and there were rats outside, cockroaches inside, and ants everywhere. I know Russ thought to himself what has my pastor gotten me into? Even Shaju found the accommodations so appalling he called his sister, Sheena (a teaching doctor in Trivandrum), to see if there was room at her house for us to sleep. We discovered upon our arrival that we would be staying in the area for the weekend, so we needed a place to stay for two nights! It was then Indian hospitality showed itself in a very Biblical way:

> Use hospitality one to another without grudging. (I Peter 4:9)

Of course, we could stay with her and her husband Joe (also a doctor) and their son Sam!

After Russ's first Indian lunch, we were off to Joe and Sheena's house to settle in before our first Church visit. We had hardly walked into the door when we heard what would be the most asked question of the trip: where is Marnie? My daughter had traveled to India with me in 2007 and had followed up that visit with a visit of her own in 2008. Marnie had visited Sheena, Joe, and Sam on a number of occasions and they had as had so many others fallen in love with her. Everybody assumed that Marnie would be returning with me (Marnie would have loved to have traveled back to India, but her graduate schedule at Dallas Theological Seminary wouldn't permit it). Whether at the homes of dear friends or at the area churches wherever Russ and I traveled in his two weeks in Kerala, the question was the same: Where in the world is Marnie? As I pondered this relationship between saints and strangers I was reminded of these lines:

> Beloved, thou doest faithfully whatsoever thou doest to brethren, and to strangers; which have borne witness of thy charity before the church: whom if thou bring forward on their journey after a godly sort, thou shalt do well: because that for His name's sake they went forth, taking nothing of the Gentiles. We therefore ought to receive such, that we might be fellowhelpers to the truth. (III John 5–8)

The Simon family of Kerala certainly fulfilled this admonition to a couple of strangers from America, in more ways than one!

2

Asking an Indian Question to an American Pastor

BY THE FRIDAY AFTERNOON of our first day in India, Russ and I were leaving Kerala for the neighboring state of Tami Nadu to see the ministry of Pastor L. Lawrence at Tholaday and Vanniyoor. I had met Pastor Lawrence in 2006, but didn't get a chance to visit his churches. One of my goals for this third trip was to finish visiting the churches of the Independent Gospel Baptist Churches of India. This small church organization had been started by Shaju's father thirty years before, and by the time of my visit numbered 19 local assemblies of believers in two states: Kerala and Tamil Nadu.

Kerala and Tami Nadu share the southern tip of India. I had visited central Tami Nadu in 2006, but not these two churches directly across the border from Trivandrum. We were schedules to have a service at Vanniyoor that night, but because of a local festival the meeting was canceled in order not to conflict with the people in the community. Pastor Lawrence was at his secondary job, a guard at a rail station, so we could only enjoy the hospitality of his wife and being shown the church buildings by Binu and Shaju. Both structures were primitive and in much need of repair. Pastor Lawrence's father had begun the work at Tholaday 50 years before and at Vanniyoor 24 years earlier. The churches had fallen on hard times with Tholaday actually closing. Lawrence had reopened Tholaday since my last visit along with pastoring Vanniyoor. Two isolated Christian communities surrounded by countless Hindu temples and Moslem mosques.

As we traveled back and forth (it took us three hours to navigate the 30 mile), I experienced some 'reaping what you sow' questions from my traveling companion. My first visit to India was highlighted by an unending stream of questions to my Indian host. Everything was so new to me, and I wanted to know of the 'why' and the 'what' that I saw. Before we even left Trivandrum, Russ was asking similar questions. Because Binu was driving (in India you need to focus on driving) and had trouble understanding English anyway, Russ's only outlet for his questions was either Shaju or myself. Shaju seemed to be on his cell phone most of the time dealing with his responsibility as National Director of the IGBC leaving me to answer Russ's endless enquiries. I now know what Solomon felt like when the Queen of Sheba showed up "to prove him with hard questions." (I Kings 10:1)

This trip to India was a big step for my carpenter friend; talk about walking outside your comfort zone; talk about 'enlarging your coast'? Before India Russ hadn't traveled far enough a field to have a passport. To say that he was experiencing a third-world country for the first time was a reality beyond description. His first fascination was the roadways and in particular the motorcycles on those highways. Russ loves motorbikes and rides regularly. Then there was the countless combinations of street vendors and roadside markets to contend with and 'what was that' and why do they do that'? I knew most of the answers to Russ's questions because I had asked the same questions during my two previous adventures. I did feel like Solomon at times and answered him all his questions (I Kings 10:3), and when I didn't know the answer I told Russ to ask Shaju; who, as before, was gracious enough to reply the best he could. As the question and answer session went on into late afternoon, I was reminded of Jesus at twelve when he confronted the scribes in the Temple:

Both hearing them, and asking them questions. (Luke 2:46)

If my Indian friends would tolerate Russ's and my questions, why do we think the Almighty will not tolerate our questions?

Call unto me, and I will answer thee, and shew thee great and mighty things, which thou knowest not! (Jeremiah 33:3)

A promise I have claimed for many a year, and a promise the Almighty will keep for you as well!

3

A Bug in the Grout

EACH AND EVERY TIME I have traveled to India I have experienced the overwhelming vastness of not only the world I live in, but the land of India itself. I have always been impressed with my world from 35,000 feet. An illustration came to me as Russ and I settled in for our first night's sleep since reaching Kerala.

After a quick trip to Tami Nadu, we were back in the home of Sheena and Joe for supper, a short visit, and bed. Russ and I had missed our Thursday night rest, and despite sleeping well on our Qatar flights, we were exhausted by the end of our first day in Kerala. They call it 'jet lag', but for me it is simply not getting my nine-hours of daily quietness. The nearer I get to sixty (I would start into my 60th year before this trip was over), the more I realize I need my sleep and more if possible. I still remember my early years in the ministry when I had a full-time job outside the church. I lived for many years on six or seven hours sleep per night with few if any days off per year. I still take few days off, but I covet dearly my 9 to 10 hours each night to rest, refresh, and recover. In the marathon that would be India 2010, I knew that a good night's sleep each night would be the key to my survival. On that first night in India the Lord would provide a quiet home, an air-conditioned room, and a valuable spiritual lesson!

It was the Psalmist David who asked:

What is man, that thou art mindful of him? (Psalms 8:4)

India is a land of bugs. Because of the heat and humidity, insects of every shape and size are found everywhere including the best homes in

Trivandrum. As I prepared for an over due slumber time, I was setting on the edge of my bed when I noticed it crawling across the floor. You must understand that the finer homes in India are made with the best of materials, including granite floors; beautiful tiles of polished granite carefully grouted together. The small lanes between each section of granite are like a highway for bugs as they make their way through and in the home. It might have been because I had been awake for over 24-hours, but suddenly I was fixated on a single, tiny bug working its way in and out of the grout through the tiles under my feet. I watched it go this way and that way as if it was lost not knowing which way to go. Then I noticed the scale of its journey there in the open of the second story bedroom Russ and I were sharing that night. Then I thought:

"Is that how the Almighty sees me?"

The bug reminded me of something that had happened that morning at the MoonStar motel. My mother-in-law, Opal Meister, had made Russ and I some molasses cookies and potato doughnuts for our trip. We had broken into this sweet treat in Doha and again in Trivandrum. When we left our motel room for breakfast that morning, I had forgotten to put a package of doughnuts away. When we returned from breakfast the local ant colony had discovered the treasure and had moved thousands of their collector ants into the container. Needless to say Russ wasn't impressed and neither was I, but all I could see was the milling throngs of India as they swarm after anything that will provide for them. Are we in the eyes of God just small creatures lost in the vastness of our world?

It was then I was reminded of the other question David asked in his classic psalm:

"And the son of man, that thou visitest him?"

Then like a thunder bolt it struck me that the God that the universe can't hold condescended to become small like me. That for thirty plus years Jesus wandered on 'earth as the poorest of them'; talk about "coasts", from the coast of heaven to the coast along the Mediterranean Sea! Limited by the restraints of time and distance, Jesus became one of us and in becoming one of us died for us and gave us an example to follow as we journey in and out of our daily grout!

4

Unexpected Stay in Trivandrum

OUR SECOND FULL-DAY IN India was divided between tourist things and ministry things. India has always been full of surprises for me. Despite the advance schedule sent to me by Shibu (Shaju's brother and president of the India ministry), I was immediately surprised when Shaju told us that we would be staying in the Trivandrum area for our first weekend in Kerala. Once I realized we were not heading directly to Kangazha, I began to understand just how the Good Lord was answering one of my India prayers (finishing visiting all the church of the IGBC) and at the same time bringing Russ face to face with a man he had personally helped.

Because our first service wasn't until that evening, Binu and Shaju had time to show us around Trivandrum, the biggest city in Kerala State. I had traveled in and out of Trivandrum four times now, but hadn't stayed in the city for long. After a breakfast of eggs, English toast, pomegranates, and bananas, we headed off to Kovalam Beach to show Russ the Indian Ocean (another part of my enlarged coast). The fifteen mile trip took us about an hour, but the trip was worth every minute to me. This would be my 3rd visit to the best beach in the world; at least according to me! I had fallen in love with this pleasant coastline on my first trip and had brought my daughter back to this white-sand shore a year later. I wanted Russ to experience the warm water, the hot sand, and the cooler breezes before the heat and humidity of the mainland overwhelmed him; and that there was one place in India that would remind him of his beloved coastline of Maine.

Our stroll along Eve's Beach, our picture in front of Kovalam Lighthouse, our wading into the high surf was all I expected and hoped for when after an hour we headed back into town. Shaju and Binu were taking us to the Trivandrum Planetarium, but on the way we saw our first elephant of the trip. Russ was the first to spot the lumbering giant walked up a side lane near the road we were traveling. Russ was excited to seen the elephant and its trainer in heavy, big-city traffic; something you never see in Ellsworth!

Our stop at the planetarium lasted about an hour and was pretty primitive by western standards, but I did have a good time talking to a youth pastor, Sujin Rai, who had brought about 50 of his kids to the show. Of course, it had an evolutionary slant, but for me the grounds with all the beautiful flowers and the air force museum next door helped make up for the lack of spiritual insight on behave of the staff of the planetarium. We took plenty of pictures, and had a good, if not a great meal at a local restaurant where I had celery soup, white bread without butter, and ice cream! We returned to our Trivandrum home for a shower and a needed rest from the heat of the day (100 plus).

That Saturday night Russ and I visited with the saints at the Narani and Ooruttambalam Baptist Churches; both pastored by T. P. Sachai. I had a chance in 2007 to visit the Ooruttambalam Church and the home of Pastor Sachai and his wife with my daughter Marnie. I had their son Libin in my classes at Kerala Baptist Bible College in 2006. I had never preached in either of the churches, so it was nice to share with the two assembles (The Missing 'ALL' of the Great Commission and The God of Hope). The highlight of the evening was for Russ to meet Pastor Sachai and his bike. In 2009 Russ headed up a fund raising endeavor to buy Pastor Sachai a motorcycle. Now Russ was able to shake hands with and speak face to face with a man he had helped in his ministry for nearly two years now, and fulfill Paul precept:

For we are labourers together with God … (I Corinthians 3:9)

Even when you are a half a world apart, and located on a different coast!

5

Russ's Amazing Race

When plans for the 2010 trip to India were in the development stages, there were a dozen or so individuals who showed interest in the project. The Venmony Church building went through many ups and downs and delays (the project would eventually take four-years from my first visit in 2006 to my last visit in 2010), and with each change in the schedule and the date of completion the lives of the individuals that wanted to go changed. My daughter Marnie had first come up with the idea of taking a group, but before she could go she was off to graduate school. Others had family situation that changed while others health concerns. When it was all said and done only Russ and I would go, but there was a time when it appeared that Russ wouldn't go either.

Feeling it was important to have one of the deacons of the Emmanuel Baptist Church (the sponsor of this building project) be there at the dedication, Russ felt lead to be that one. Shortly after he made that decision he was laid off from his job. Russ Coffin is a carpenter by trade, but a builder of ships by occupation. His boat company, Hinckley Boats, was going through a hard time with the down-turn in the economy, and one of the first to be laid off was Russ. Now Russ had the time but not the money. An appeal to the Church family soon resulted in Russ having the money, and then, six-months later, Russ was hired back. He now had the money but not the time. After much prayer and thought, Russ decided to tell his boss about the India trip, and ask for the two weeks off he needed. All I can think of is what happened to Nehemiah when he asked for some time off from his job to do a work for God in a distant land (Nehemiah 2:1–8). Nehemiah would go to Jerusalem and Russ would go to Venmony.

Enlarge My Coast

One of my favorite reality shows currently on television is The Amazing Race. A show that pits teams of two on a round the world adventure to see which team can complete the race first. One of the first characteristic I have noticed about the teams that win the race is their compatibility. When I knew Russ and I would travel half-way around the world together, live together for two weeks, and face unknown challenges, I knew I could do it with Russ because I knew this about Russ and me from Psalms 133:1:

> "Behold, how good and how pleasant it is
> for brethren to dwell together in unity."

I had been Russ's pastor nearly 19 years before we departed on our Amazing Race. We had also fished together on a number of fishing trips into the Northern Maine Woods. As a matter of fact, one of the first trips I ever took after becoming the pastor of the Emmanuel Baptist Church was a five day canoe/fishing trip into a backwater lake only accessible by canoe. Russ was my companion and guide then, and I knew from that trip alone we could survive very well together no matter the race.

Russ had also been a deacon for many years by the time we boarded our plane for India, and through countless deacon's meetings and workdays at the church we were of one-mind and one-purpose most of the time. That ageless concept of Amos would work very well with us:

> Can two walk together, except they be agreed? (Amos 3:3)

We would win The Amazing Race: India because we were compatible companions in Christ!

6

A Caribbean Marnie

OUR LAST DAY IN Trivandrum was Sunday. Our schedule called for a morning service at the Kachani Baptist Church and an afternoon trip (100 miles north) to Edayappara for an evening welcome service at the Kangazha Baptist Church.

After a family picture and breakfast with Sheena, Joe, and Sam, we said goodbye to our gracious hosts. Their home was an oasis for us in the hot and hustle that is a typical Indian city. I am still amazed how people survive in the climate and the culture of the masses. Russ and I had already seen more people in two days than we would see in an entire year in Ellsworth, and we had already endured temperatures we will never see in Maine! That is why I have always found 'Melita" (Acts 28:1) such a place of refuge. (Indian families name their homes, and Sheena and Joe named theirs after the island Paul and his shipwrecked companions found safety from the terrible Mediterranean storm they endured-interestingly Melita means 'refuge'!)

Pastor Paul and his people at the Kachani Church were as friendly and welcoming as they were the first time I had visited them four years before. It was at this every same church I had my last service during my 2006 trip. I spoke on God's Unspeakable Gift (II Corinthians 9:15) and Russ gave his testimony. After the service a pretty girl came up to us, and of course asked, "Where is Marnie?" She had meet Marnie at KBBC while Marnie was teaching there in 2008. She had that same infectious smile and bubbling personality that Marnie has. She reminded me of a young lady Russ and I met and got to know on our first Qatar flight. I can't remember whether it was me or Russ who labeled her 'a Caribbean Marnie'?

Enlarge My Coast

Her name was Stacey and she was from Trinidad (another coastal person). She was on her way to India for a month stay in Goa, a small tourist area on India's western coast. What drew me to this young lady was the fact we would be sitting beside each other for nearly twelve hours, or so we thought. As we settled into our seats, she told me of the round the world adventure she was on. She had just spent a month in South America, and when she returned from India she would be traveling to Europe for a month before being off to Asia for a month! (I never figured out whether she was rich or had rich parents?) As she told me of her plans her pleasant personality and friendly nature came through that infectious smile and bubbling demeanor. It was then we noticed that there were no passengers in the three sets ahead of us. It was then we noticed the plane was nearly half empty. A long story short, she was able to move up to the three seats in front of where I sat, and I in turn would have three seats to myself. Without a doubt the best airplane flight I have ever taken (I slept 8 hours uninterrupted and fully laid out)! We last saw Stacey at Doha as we went through customs, but our brief encounter will always be apart of my India trip 2010 memory.

At Kachani I meet an Indian Marnie, and it seems that no matter how far I roam I meet people that remind me of my daughter. Even Russ commented on the characteristics of the young ladies we were meeting. It was hard to say goodbye to the people of India each and every time we met. Our visits were so short, but there were other 'marnies' to see, as we took the MC (Main Coast) Road north. I saw big improvement to this road, for the last time I traveled on it our journey took five hours while this time only three. We arrived at Edayappara just in time for supper. The entire Simon family was there to greet us, and once again the kids (Joshua, Abigail, and Jerry) all wanted to know where Marnie was. I told them I had to leave her behind this time, but I was sure she would return!

Wherever Marnie has traveled she has taken on the culture, and without a doubt there is 'an African Marnie', a Slovakian Marnie, and an Indian Marnie! Marnie believes in Paul's philosophy (I Corinthians 9:19-22):

> ...I am made all things to all men, that I might by all means save some. And this I do for the gospel sake, that I might be partaker thereof with you.
> (I Corinthians 9:22-23)

No matter, what 'coast' you find yourself?

7

John's Funeral

ON SUNDAY FEBRUARY 21, 2010, I arrived back in my Indian 'hometown'. It had been nearly three years since I left this peaceful hamlet situated deep in the Kerala hills. One of the reason I have come to love Edayappara is the rural atmosphere and neighborly attitude of the people of that place; very similar to my hometown of Perham, Maine. It was a joy to introduce Russ to my many friends and spiritual brothers and sisters as we settled into our home away from home for the next two weeks.

First, we stopped at Shaju's house and had supper (fried chicken but without the heavy spices that normally accompanies an Indian meal). Once again my favorite Indian cook (Shaju's mother Annamma) prepared an American meal with Indian ingredients. Since my first stay at their house, I have been treated as a king and during my third visit nothing changed. After supper we were off to the Kangazha Church next door for our welcoming service, but this time combined with the monthly communion service for the college students of Kerala Baptist Bible College. It was here I meet again some of the orphans from the Mercy Children's Home; kids I had gotten to know on my first and second visits to Kerala. I also got to see again some of the students I had taught in 2006, and of course, some of my pastor friends and college professor friends. It was also at this gathering we were suddenly informed of the passing of M. J. John. Once again our predetermined schedule was going to be changed and abated (The Good Lord seemed to be altering our plans for His own as He often does in our lives.)!

I had met M. J. (Many Indian believers are renamed after their conversion accepting Biblical names like John. Only the first letters of their old Hindu names are retained.) John four years before. For me, John will always be remembered as the security guard for KBBC and an all around helpful, handyman to the students of the college. He also could be found helping his dear wife Mary, the chief cook at the school. They both worked tirelessly to not only meet the needs of the students and staff of KBBC, but to see that they were kept safe and secure. I knew John would leave a big hole at the college, and his significance was know when Shibu announced at the end of the communion service that all activities at KBBC would be suspended until after John's funerals.

Indian funeral usually take place within 24-hours after a departure. The body is prepared at home and the family members stay around the body until the funeral. To my surprise, the next morning I was asked to participate in the service at the home. There are actually three separate services: one at the person's home, one at the local church, and one at the burial site. The body would be literally carried from site to site. By 1 PM a large crowd had gathered at Mary's house about a mile from the church. I was ushered to the front row with the other pastors who would participate. I shared:

> Blessed are the dead which die in the Lord from henceforth.
> (Revelation 14:13)

After an hour of singing, praying and sharing, we slowing walked John's body to the Kangazha Church were we had more singing and sharing and scripture reading. After nearly another hour, we walked back to the cemetery which was located right next door to Mary's house. You got to understand we did this in 118 degree heat and high humidity. Finally after three hours we put John's body to rest in the church tomb at the Edayappara cemetery. I had just experienced another first in India; perhaps, the saddest first of all!

8

A Scooter for Pastor Paul

ALL REGULARLY SCHEDULED EVENTS at KBBC had been suspended on the first day of Bible Conference and Graduation week because of the unexpected passing of trustee M. J. John. It wasn't until that evening that the activities of KBBC began with an area-wide evangelistic service in the courtyard of the school. But before that service began, Russ and I had a very special present from the people of Emmanuel Baptist to deliver.

Another one of the reason that Russ Coffin joined me on this India trip was to see for himself what was being done with a very special project he had directed for nearly four years. When I returned to Emmanuel in 2006, one of the needs of India I presented was for transportation for Indian pastors. I had discovered on my tour of the area churches that most of the pastors didn't even live in the village they were pastoring in. One of the reasons I wanted to build a parsonage (the first ever built in the IGBC) was to give the pastors a chance to live where they pastored. I discovered that most pastors in the organization had to take public transportation from where they lived to where they worked, and sometimes that was many, many miles away. Because of the unreliability of the Indian bus system a motorcycle would help cut down on travel time. I share the need with the church family and Russ (the motorcycle lover that he is) felt this was a way to help the pastors of Kerala and beyond.

Almost immediately, he raised enough money in 2007 so a new motorcycle could be presented to Pastor Thomas when Marnie went to India to teach in 2008. In 2008, Russ thought he would try again and before the year was through had enough money to buy a second bike for a pastor (Sake Matthews) in Andrah Pardesh. The success of the program saw

15

another bike purchased and presented to Pastor Sachai (the one we visited in Trivandrum) in 2009. As we prepared for our 2010 trip Russ was not only raising money for his own trip, but money for a 4th motorcycle and a 4th pastor. This time he wanted to make the presentation personally, and after supper on our first Monday in India the stage was set for another amazing presentation.

The twist in this motorcycle delivery was the history of the pastor to receive the gift. Each and every time Russ would get enough funds together (monetary gifts from church members, friends, and Russ's own handiwork; Russ would make wooden articles and sell them with the funds going into the bike ministry) we would contact Shibu and see who was in the most need of a motorcycle. Each time Shibu and his staff would prayerfully consider who should receive the gift. I had also met all the recipients, so it was nice to know who the bikes were going to. For the 2010 gift Pastor Paul was chosen. But Pastor Paul was one of the older pastors, and he had never driven a motorcycle before. It was decided that instead of a motorcycle, a scooter would be bought. This scooter would be automatic and much easier to run and ride. Most of the pastors would be at the Bible Conference anyway, so it wasn't difficult to call Pastor Paul to Shaju's house just before the evening service and not give away the purpose of the call. He thought he was coming just to see us again. Little did he know what was in store for him?

I wish I could describe the expression on Pastor Paul's face when Russ, through a translator, told him of the gift Emmanuel wanted to give him. After we make the formal presentation of the keys, we took him outside where Binu had the new scooter waiting. Interestingly, when the presentation was over, two of the four bikes Russ had given over the years were in the church yard, for Pastor Thomas had come to the conference on his bike:

> He that giveth let him do it with simplicity.
> (Romans 12:8)

9

Old Messages and Old Friends

SHORTLY AFTER WE PRESENTED Pastor Paul with his new scooter, Russ and I were off to the first service of the 2010 KBBC Bible Conference. I had the privilege to share during a similar conference in 2007, so I was ready for the length of service, the heat despite the darkness, and the strange artificial lights. For Russ, it was his first experience in an open-air setting, and the overpowering attraction that a white-man has in India.

My first message was an old standby I had been preaching for years: Why Should You Accept Christ Today? Based in Hebrews 4:7:

> To day if you hear His voice, harden not your hearts.

One of the joys of going far a field to preach and teach is the ability to pull out old messages and preach or teach them again. When you have been a pastor at the same church for 18 years it is difficult to preach an old message. Even a preacher enjoys preaching some messages over again, so to get a chance to dust off an old sermon card (I have since 1979 put ever sermon I have ever prepared on a 4 by 6 card. As a matter of fact, just before we went to India together Russ had finished making me a custom-made, pine cabinet containing five drawers that I could put all my sermon and study notes in one place. He built it so all my 4 by 6 cards could fit neatly in these drawers. It is a wealth of spiritual and Biblical information that helps with each and every new sermon or study I prepare. It also gives me instant access to subject matters for trips like to India!). Each and every sermon I preached in India (I would preach or teach 49 times in 30 days) was an old message revived for the setting and situation I found in Kerala, or elsewhere.

Also on that first evening ministering in India I was also able to get together once again with some old friends. People that I had met in previous trips; individuals that I had stayed in touch with over the three year separation. I am always humbled by the distance some of these friends come to see me again. A case in point was a young man by the name of Jaldev. I had met Jaldev in 2006. He was one of my four seniors in the class of '06. We seemed to have an immediate connection. After graduation from KBBC, Jaldev decided to return to KBBC for their master's program. It was my wife and my honor to pay for those two years of schooling, another aspect that brought us closer. I had continued to follow his ministry when he returned to his home state of Chhattisgarh, in central India. Since I had seen him last he had married, had a baby girl, and had started working with his father in their hometown of Bastar and the surrounding communities. On the first night of our evangelistic crusade in Edayappara guess who showed up?

There in the crowd was Jaldev, his wife, an aunt, his daughter, and his father. They had traveled nearly 800 miles to see me and to enjoy the KBBC Bible Conference. It reminded me of the time when I went back to be graduation speaker for the class of 2007 that another one of my seniors from 2006 traveled nearly 300 miles with her daughter and new-born son, Emanuel, to see me again. Rotni (she now lives at Asia Christian Academy where she works at the library while her children go to school) and her husband are missionaries to the Nepal people in Tamil Nadu today. And then if Jaldev's visit wasn't enough, in the crowd before the week was over was another 2006 student who was doing his graduate work in a Bible school in Tamil Nadu; he traveled over 100 miles to see me. Moses (at the writing of this book Moses is in his last year of graduate work and would finish his training at Asia Christian Academy in 2012) was also a young man I had been able to help in his schooling over the years:

> Ointment and perfume rejoice the heart: so doth the sweetness
> of a man's friend... (Proverbs 27:9)

I have many friends in India, and the sweetness of their presence is a joy every time.

10

Handing Out Awards at Bethany School

Russ and I started our fifth day in India with an early morning walk to some of my favorite places in Edayappara. I discovered on my other trips to India that the best time of the day to venture outside was either early in the morning or after dark. Because after dark was a no-no for the Simon's guests, early morning was the accepted time for a walk!

Our first destination was to Big Stream, my old baptism hole. The mission has since built a baptistery behind Bethany School, but for me my Jordan River is the creek that runs through the rubber tree fields east of town. On the way we watched as a couple of lumber merchants measured a few big logs along the roadside. We also ran into Joy Thomas on his way to the market for milk. There were a few rubber tree workers taping trees, so Russ got a chance to see this aspect of Kerala. The stream was nearly dry, as I show him the place I had one of my most thrilling experiences in India: the baptism of six people including Julie Simon's mother, Daisy. As we walked back the way we had come, the heat began to affect our pace. It was well over 80 heading for another 100 plus day. The humidity was also soaring as we walked by the orphanage. It was nice to see the kids again, but was disappointed to discover that some of my Indian children had moved away, especially my 'gate-keeper', Nidhin C. Ramesh. We got back to the Simon home just in time for breakfast: sausage, eggs, and English toast (bread toasted in lots of butter on a grill)! Julie never once made us an Indian breakfast; she had lived in the United States for many years and knew what Americans like for the most important meal of the day.

Enlarge My Coast

After breakfast we were off for the first session of the Bible Conference. My theme for the meetings was 'The Man of God' (I Timothy 6:11). I preached twice on the subject in the morning and afternoon sessions. The two meetings were split by lunch. At Annamma's Russ and I enjoyed hamburgers, French fries, and ice cream for dessert. Russ was questioning whether or not we were in India? It was around Annamma's table that Russ and I were asked if we might have some free time later in the afternoon. The request came from Julie Simon (Shaju's wife and director of the Bethany Medium School). One of the big ministries of the Simon family in Edayappara is this private Christian school. Began by Annamma in the early 1990's, this school would be equal to our private elementary schools in the States. Nearly 300 students attend this school, and only recently had Annamma given up the position of director because of her age. Her daughter-in-law had taken over, and she was looking for some special American guests to handout awards at a school assembly. Russ and I were quick to volunteer for the job!

Later that afternoon, after the Bible Conference meeting, Russ and I headed across town to Bethany. On the way we stopped at the main office of the ministry to see Binu. One of the blessings Russ and I had on this trip was to give away monetary funds that had been given to us to meet a need we found. A couple in our church had given us some funds and we thought that new tires were in order for Shaju's ministry car. We had noticed in our travels in Trivandrum the lack of rubber on Shaju's wheels. Binu, the official driver of the mission, was responsible for the care for the vehicles attached to the ministry. We gave him enough money to put a new set of tires on Shaju's car. I remembered the last time I was in India I did the same for Shibu's car. Once that task was complete we walked through the brutal Indian heat to the Bethany Christian Medium School for a late afternoon assembly.

Over the next two hours Russ and I handed out over 300 awards in sports, music, art, and other special accomplishments.

...and in that thou givest a reward..." (Ezekiel 16:34)

It was one of the highlights of our trip to listen to the children sing, and witness the brown smiles. Both Russ and I had our digital cameras and plenty of pictures and photographs were taken to help us remember our special afternoon. It was better than the Emmys or Oscars, or you would have thought so by the reaction of the children as we handed them their certificates and simple prizes!

11

Three Days of Sermons

I HAVE ALWAYS BELIEVED in the admonition of Paul:

> Preach the word; be instant in season, out of season; reprove, rebuke, exhort with all longsuffering and doctrine. (II Timothy 4:2)

Over a three day period in Edayappara, I was able to practice this instruction three times each day.

The week before graduation at KBBC was divided up into two distinct categories: instruction and evangelism. The morning and afternoon meetings were given over to teaching and study for the Bible students, the college staff, and the local pastors that could attend the sessions. The evening service was open to the community and had a distinct Gospel theme to it. I had the privilege of being the main speaker at all of these meeting. I had come with a battle plan and this is how it all worked out.

My first message in "The Man of God" series was concerning 'the man of God' in the word, and what the 'word' will do: convert him, communicate to him, convict him, correct him, change him, complete him, and commission him (II Timothy 3:15–17). The second message challenged 'the man of God' during weariness: weary in the battle, but never weary of the battle; weary in the trial, but never weary of the trial; weary in the fight, but never weary of the fight; weary in the journey, but never weary of the journey, and weary in the ministry, but never weary of the ministry (Psalms 6:6). The third message dealt with 'the man of God' and his walk: a man who will be quiet enough to hear God's message; a man who is courageous enough to herald God's message, and a man who is honest enough to heed

God's message (I John 2:6). The forth message in the series highlighted 'the man of God' and his work: the man needs to be appointed, anointed, authorized, apologetic, and affectionate (I Corinthians 1:18–23). The fifth message underlined 'the man of God' in the spiritual warfare of life: as a son, a sower, a student, a scholar, a sprinter, and as a soldier (II Timothy 2:1–15). The final message in this series of instruction placed 'the man of God' in the world: when battling anarchy, he must stay alert; when battling apostasy, he must stay authentic; and when battling apathy, he must stay awake (II Corinthians 15:34). I used in these messages those men who the Bible calls 'men of God' as illustrations:

> Timothy (I Timothy 6:11), Elisha (II Kings 4:9), Elijah (I Kings 17:24), David (II Chronicles 8:14), Samuel (I Samuel 9:6), Moses (Deuteronomy 33:1), and Shemaiah (I Kings 12:22)!

For my evangelistic messages, I chose three old favorites. On Monday night I preached on "Why Should You Accept Christ Today?" based on Hebrews 4:7. I gave these three reason: Christ saves today (II Corinthians 6:2), Christ satisfies today (John 3:36), and Christ secures today (John 10:28–29). On Tuesday night I preached on "People Grow Better In Grace (I Corinthians 15:9–11). I shared these three illustrations: the attributes of God, the actions of Paul, and the abundance of labor. On Wednesday night, the last night of the crusade, I preached on "A Greater Than Solomon Is Here" (Matthew 12:42). I made these ten comparisons to King Solomon and our Saviour:

> …greater in His position, possessions, power, performance, preaching, philosophy, promises, proclamations, provision, and peace.

Each night an invitation was give, but nobody responded. Other messages and many responses were still ahead for me!

12

The Regions Beyond

OUR FIRST WEEK IN India was passing quickly as our days were filled with meetings and meeting old friends and making new ones. I especially enjoyed getting to know the new and very young men that were taking responsibility at KBBC and the area churches (Pastor George had replaced Pastor P.P. Mathai at Kangazha following a stroke.). I was sad to see Professor Matthew probably for the last time (and it was the last time this side of heaven for my friend passed away just a year after our last meeting at the early age of 56). We had become close friends and colleagues because of our love of church history. Poor health was causing him to retire after graduation from KBBC. He would return to his home church in Payappadg (about five miles from Edayappara) and go back to pastoring.

Two young teachers at KBBC stood out to me. JoJo Matthews translated for me during one of the sessions and I loved his pleasant manner and wonderful smile. John Adam David (John: the name of a brother who had died, Adam: his given name, and David: his father's name) was a young man Marnie told me to look up. She had met him while teaching at KBBC, and I found him as friendly and interesting as she said. He also translated for me during one of the sessions, a very difficult task. I also had a chance to meet with Jaldev and his father for a long discussion on their ministry in Bastar. The ministry was expanding through their thirteen churches and the orphanage ministry was also growing. It was nice to get caught up with his life, family, and ministry.

Perhaps, the best joy of all was my meeting with the "Torchbearers" (interestingly, it was my daughter who gave them their name in 2008). Abinas Khaka, Gopel Digal, and Sarat Digal were three young men I had in my classes in 2006. One of the reasons I wanted to return for graduation 2010 was these three students. To see them four years later graduate was a highlight of my ministry to India. All from the State of Assam in northern India; they were returning to develop a ministry to the unreached villages of their state. They had dedicated their summers in laying the groundwork for this ministry, and now it was time to go out on their own. When I pray for them I am reminded of a hymn they taught me in 2006 called "The Regions Beyond" (the unofficial theme song for me while at Kerala Baptist Bible College):

> "To the regions beyond I must go, I must go, where the story has never been told; to the millions that never have heard of His love, I must tell the sweet story of old. To the hardest of places He calls me to go, not thinking of comfort or ease; the world may pronounce me a dreamer, a fool, enough if the Master I please. O ye that are spending your leisure and powers in pleasures so foolish and fond. Awake from your selfishness, folly, and sin and go to the regions beyond. There are other lost sheep that the Master must bring, and to them must the message be told. He sends me to gather them out of all lands and welcome them back to His fold. To the regions beyond, I must go, I must go. Till the world, all the world, His salvation shall know!"

Albert and Margaret Simpson wrote this song during the height of the missionary movement of the 19th century. It is such a joy to be around young people that still sense the need and urgency of the time. In my nearly forty years in the pastorate, I have had the privilege of having only a handful of young adults desire to give themselves in full-time missionary service, yet in my short four year experience in India it has been more like handfuls of young men and women who have such a desire. I have worried for years that there will be a shortage of future Christian leaders in the United States, but I have no such worry for India! The Great Commission is still alive and well in that land:

> Go ye therefore, and teach all nations, baptizing them ... teaching them to observe all things ... and, lo, I am with you always, even to the end of the world ... (Matt. 28:19–20)

And these young people are not afraid to go 'To the Regions Beyond', for me, just another definition for 'enlarge my coast'![1]

---

1. I published a book in 2012 with the same title based on my 1972 trip to a region beyond in the country of Australia. I was inspired to relive that spiritual adventure in words by the testimony of the young missionaries I meet in India!

13

Cooking Pancakes over an Open Fire

THE LAST DAY OF Bible Conference brought additional surprises for Russ and me!

It started after another restful night's sleep. The blessing of India is the hundred degrees (it would hit 122 on this day) days do not reach into the night. Once the sun sets it cools off nicely, and even the humidity seems to diminish. During the morning and afternoon sessions, I finished my "The Man of God" series, and there would be no evening evangelistic service. A new tradition for graduation week had been established since my last visit in 2007: an annual staff barbecue, Indian style?

Around the breakfast table Shibu told us of the evening gathering of staff and friends planned for after dark. It would be a time of fellowship, fun, and food as the academic year came to a close. When Shibu had built his home, he created a huge patio area in the back of the house under the overhang of the back section of the structure. It made an ideal place for large gatherings. I still remember the day he told me why he had built this building the way he did. He told of his fear that one day Christianity might be forced underground like our brothers and sisters in China. He wanted a place away from the church building where the saints could gather. I must admit that I have never thought in those terms, never dreaming that wholesale persecution would ever come to America, yet in India, you must always prepare, even in the stable State of Kerala!

Before the big gathering took place, Russ and I had a chance to go into Partathanam and exchange some money and see a few sites. Since our arrival in Edayappara we had pretty much been limited in our travels to the village itself. Even though we only went down the road a couple of miles it was like going into an entirely new area. Partathanam is a much bigger village with a huge market area and plenty of small businesses. We were able to get 45.7 rupees for every American greenback (we only got 40.4 at the airport in Trivandrum). On the way back to the college, we stopped at an Indian sawmill to see where Shibu got his furniture made for his new house (All the wood for all the furniture came from one huge teak tree they had removed from behind his mother's home!). It was eye opening to see the primitive methods still used in India to saw wood and make furniture. Very labor intensive, the process might be slow, but the end produce is the best I have ever seen (Russ loved the visit because he is a cabinet builder by trade; he builds the galleys for Hinckley Boats)! Interestingly, the owner of the mill was a Moslem, but very friendly and very proud to show us his business.

Around seven o'clock, the staff and the families of KBBC began to gather behind Shibu's home. I helped Shibu start a campfire in a pit lined with concrete blocks. I was encouraged for I pictured roasting hot dogs and other campfire food, but I knew better. Often I forget I am in a foreign land when I travel. This would not be a typical barbecue, and deep down I knew it. Once the fire was hot Binu, who I learned that night had just been named the new purchasing manager for the mission, put a huge round, steel plate over the fire and began cooking what looked like pancakes. At the same time Shibu had a two hole gas grill fired up and he began making omelets. While talking to the staff I learned that Asia Christian Academy in Tamil Nadu was connected to Dallas Theological Seminary (where my daughter is studying), and that another former student of mine, Moses Digar, was studying there (another member of the Torchbearers). As Julie brought out the extras for this Indian Barbecue I realized I was a long way away from Texas and the best barbecue I had ever had. Despite the poor food the fellowship was sweet; reminding me of these verses in Philippians:

> For your fellowship in the gospel from the first day until now ...
> if any fellowship of the Spirit ... fulfill ye my joy,
> that ye be likeminded, having the same love, being of one accord ...
> (Philippians 1:5, 2:1–2)

We might never be able to agree on the food of India, but the fellowship of India will never be debated or disagreed on. I have never been to a 'coast' where there has been such like-mindedness and love among the brethren!

14

A Bell for KBBC

ONE OF THE GREAT joys of an India ministry is the simple things one can do that will have a huge impact on so many people. After nearly six days of continual meetings, Russ and I had a chance to take a break on graduation day (February 26, 2010). The only scheduled event that day was graduation practice at eleven and the service at seven. We had the day to reflect on the whirlwind that had been our first eight-days on the road. They had flown by, but not to quick that we hadn't been able to notice a few things.

I had already started making a list of the chapters in my third India book. At this stage in our trip I thought the title would have to be: India Journey? Russ's big observation had to do with what he didn't see, or hear at the college. Despite the language barrier and the unfamiliar surrounds, Russ had come to every meeting, every service, despite the heat, and despite the downtime; Russ had hoped to use his carpentry skill to either build something or repair something while he was in India. Because of the graduation and the dedication schedule time was limited and no hands-on ministry would be forthcoming while Russ was in Kerala. I know that he was a bit disappointed, but he never showed it as he followed me from meeting to meeting. Russ had a chance on occasion to share his testimony, and give a challenge or two, but most of the time he was sitting and listening and observing!

Kerala Baptist Bible College hasn't got the modern equipment you might see on an American campus. They didn't even have a phone until after my first visit I left money to purchased the first one (Most of the students came from other states and their only means of communication (most can't afford a cell phone) with their families was by letter or phone.

Before I bought the first one they had to go over to Shaju's house, or be called to Shaju's home if a loved one or friend called.) I was glad to see since my first visit they had gotten in a few more computers, but even they are rare at KBBC. The housing situation is primitive. Despite the fact they have built a new residential building, all the boys are crammed into a few rooms on one floor. I still remember the first time we visited Abinas, Gopel, and Sarat; bunk beds side by side covering just about ever inch of space with only small walkways between the rows. Improvements had certainly been made in the library, the class rooms, the girl's dorm, and the housing for the staff, but there were still a lot of needs, and Russ spotted one almost immediately.

It wasn't however until graduation day that Russ finally voiced his observation that KBBC lacked one very important piece of equipment: a bell. For, four years I had known about the method used to call the students to class. I had witnessed the unique sound during my professor days at KBBC. Under the walkway that connects the kitchen/dormitory building with the classroom building hung a metal leaf from an old car spring. When it was time to change class somebody would pick up a stick and begin to beat the piece of metal. Because the campus sets on less than an acre of land the sound can be heard, but for Russ it didn't sound college enough. So as we walked to the Kangazha Church to practice our marching for graduation, Russ told me that before he left India KBBC would have a proper alarm, a brass bell. We had hoped to go to Kottayam on our free time that day, but Binu was busy. Nevertheless, the very next day we made the run into Kottayam and Russ purchased the biggest bell we could find. It wasn't used for graduation as he had hoped, but it is in use today. A bell that I got to hang and to hear rung before I left India three weeks after Russ had made his desire known: Russell's bell reminds me of this precept of Paul's recorded in his first letter to the Corinthians:

> And even things without life giving sound, whether pipe or harp,
> except they give a distinction in the sounds, how shall it be known
> what is piped or harped? (I Corinthians 14:7)

And could I add rung? Now there is a very distinct sound on the campus at KBBC because of the observation and generosity of a stranger from Maine, and could we say 'a Maine coastal sound.'

15

The Old Paths-Graduation Day

ON FEBRUARY 26, 2010, I had the privilege and honor of speaking to the graduation class of KBBC for the second time (my first time was on March 2, 2007). My first graduation address was for only three students, but this time I would share my challenge with 14 and hundreds of family and friends. When I first taught at KBBC, the entire student body was just 18. Today the number is 71. It was nice to see the growth, so much so, that the graduation ceremonies had to be conducted in the courtyard of the Kangazha Church verses the main sanctuary my first time there.

My address to the graduates this time centered on the truth of this inspiring verse:

> Thus saith the Lord, stand ye in the ways, and see, and ask for the old paths, where is the good way, and walk therein, and ye shall find rest for your souls. But they said, we will not walk therein. (Jeremiah 6:16)

My message focused on the crossroad these students (Grace Cham Roy, Wontim K.S., A. S. Yurshimla, Abui Newme, Narahimhas Rao, Son Kiling, Longki Rongpi, Ningsophang Raising, S. Suresh, Suraj Prasad Lama, Reisang Azyamah, Sarat Digal, Gopel Digal, and Abinas Khaka) had come to, and the decisions they must make to continue their journey.

At the heart of my sermon was the precept that 'the old paths' of Christianity are still 'the good way' today. Despite the changes in Christendom, Christ's example hasn't changed, and we can still find rest in the same manner and the same methods of old (Matthew 11:28–30). I used

First John 2:6 as the bridge between Jeremiah's concept of 'the ways' to our 'walk with Christ':

> He that saith he abideth in Him ought himself
> also so to walk, even as He walked!

I divided the message into these three parts:

1. Walking before God Implies a Holy Lifestyle —Genesis 17:1. God doesn't only want us to walk with Him, but walk like Him as well. (I Peter 1:16) We are not to walk in the new paths of morality, but in the old paths of purity. (I Timothy 4:12) Jesus set the example and the standard long, long, ago and nothing has changed, no matter what the currents trends and teachers may say!

2. Walking after God Implies Obedient Service for God—Deuteronomy 13:4. If we choose the old paths God has promised to always walk before us (Psalms 23:4), so no matter where you go God has already been there ahead of you, just like He did for the children of Israel in their travels from Egypt to Canaan. "The steps of a good man are always ordered of the Lord!" (Psalms 37:23)

3. Walking with God Implies Fellowship with God—Genesis 5:22. I believe we can add friendship to this point as well. Our God has always desired a close relationship with His children. This old path goes back to Eden (Genesis 3:8). The philosophy that God is somehow a distant sovereign is man-made, not a divine teaching. These are the old paths you must choose, and it is a choice. Note, again the context and the rejection of the people of Jeremiah to his challenge!

God has not made us robots, or zombies, but men and women of choices; if you will "coastal choices." What will you choice?

16

Saturday Blessings

Whenever I have a day like I had on our second Saturday in India, I am reminded of this precept from the pen of Paul:

> Blessed be the God and Father of our Lord Jesus Christ, who hath blessed us with all spiritual blessings in heavenly places in Christ. (Ephesians 1:3)

And could I just add, in earthly places like Kerala as well!

This special day started early with an auto (the three-wheeled carts of India) ride with Jacob John. There is no better way to see rural India than through the side-windows of a three-wheeled tri-cycle barely six-inches off the ground. Our goal was to find an elephant, and Jacob took us far a field, but we saw none. We traveled down to the river through Mundathanam, but the most exciting thing we could find that Saturday morning was a crew tarring the road on the other side of the river. I recognized a few members of the team, the same ones that were tarring through Edayappara in 2006. I showed Russ the mission's rubber tree plantation, and by the time we returned to Shibu's house it was already 90 degrees.

After fresh pineapple juice and Julie's English toast, we were off to the last chapel at KBBC for 2010. Most of the students would be catching a train for home after lunch, but there was still some unfinished business from graduation. In order to keep the graduation service shorter (it still lasted two and a half hours), some awards were held back to a final gathering of the student body. The ceremony was held on the new forth floor of the academic building. Once again Russ and I were chosen to give out the special awards to some of the students plus their transcripts for the year.

We also handed out the Teacher of the Year Award (JoJo Matthews) and Administrator of the Year Award. Interestingly, JoJo wife got this award. We got to say goodbye to the students, many we will not see again until Heaven, while others I would meets again in a few days in Andrah Pardesh.

After lunch we were off with Binu for a five hour shopping trip to Kottayam. And sure enough we hadn't gotten five miles out of town when Binu stopped the car and pointed to a huge elephant in the forest beside the road. Again the Good Lord allowed us to get up close and personal with a forest elephant gathering brush. We were able to literally walk up to the elephant and watch it at work. The last we saw of the massive creature was its back-end as it walked away from us with a huge pile of banana leaves in its trunk. And just a few minutes later when we pulled into Kottayam we saw a second elephant in a lumberyard on the outskirts of town. Again the animal seemed so large surrounded by piles of uncut logs. Each and every time I have had the privilege of seeming one of God most wonderful creations I have been blessed. This was Russ's third elephant, but another blessing on another blessed day in Kerala.

Another blessing was getting everything on our shopping list despite having to go all over town; there are no Lowe's, Home Depot, or Wal-Mart in that area of India! Each purchase was bought in a separate store, and some of those stores were very difficult to find because of traffic, or lack of parking. We eventually got a set of emergency lights for the orphanage and dining hall; a new brass bell for the college; a new toaster for Julie; new guitar straps and picks for the college guitars, and three children's outfits. The comedy of errors on this trip was watching three grown men trying to buy dresses for two little girls. That evening we had been invited to the monthly birthday party at the children's home. There were three birthday children: a boy and twin girls. The last blessing of the day was the faces of these three orphans when we gave them their gifts, matching outfits we would see modeled on dedication Sunday the next day. Any day is a blessed day when you can bring a smile to the face of an abandoned child! Amen and Amen

17

It Was Made of Bricks

THE DAY HAD FINALLY arrived after four years of dreaming, planning, giving, and traveling. It was time for Russ and me to dedicate the new Venmony Baptist Church, a gift from the people of Emmanuel Baptist.

I woke around 6:30 AM on the big day. I was excited to say the least. Today would fulfill the first actual vision I had ever received in the ministry. I am not a visionary, and I had never before experienced the insight I understood the first time I visited Venmony in 2006. When Shibu and Pastor Reji showed me the land that had been bought for a new sanctuary, I knew I was the one to lead the mission to find the funds necessary to build on that site. I had never undertaken such a project before, but I was compelled to try. Over the four years since I first understood my calling the Good Lord had supplied the funds; He had broken through all the obstacles; He had overcome all the restriction, and had overseen all the changes necessary to see the project through to completion. I had come to see the final product.

Around the breakfast table that morning, our conversion centered on the events of the day, but another strange happening in India the day before was shared by Shibu. While Russ and Binu and I were shopping in Kottayam, Shibu was at a funeral of one of the pastor's father. When they got the body to the cemetery, they discovered that the casket was too big for the brick-lined hole. Because the grave could not be changed, they literally had to cut the ends off the casket so it would fit the hole. The whole process took an hour and a half before the body could be properly buried (only in India). I told Shibu I hoped we wouldn't have any such problems in Venmony, we didn't.

Enlarge My Coast

Around 7:30 AM, we left the Simon home with two bus loads of believers from the surrounding area for the thirty mile trip to Venmony. The two hour (yes, two hour) trip took us through the tropical hills and valleys that is central Kerala. On the way we saw another forest elephant (Russ's 4th and last) walking slowly along the road just before we got to the old church (the house of a couple who now lives in the United States). There in the courtyard of the home the people were gathering from all the Independent Gospel Baptist Churches of Kerala. Shibu told me that there was at least one representative from the other 18 churches there. The crowd was growing with each passing moment, and the group that was going to feed the multitude after the dedication was already cooking the food. The plan was to actually walk the final two miles to the new church. Because of the hostility in the town towards this first church building in the community, the organization decided that it wouldn't be wise for Russ and I to walk with the group (we were very disappointed). To appease us, Shibu allowed Binu to drive Russ and me back and forth beside the crowd to get a feel of the procession. The trip from old church to new church took about two hours more. All along the way the people sang, with a small band of musicians leading the way.

By the time the five hundred people got to the new church building and parsonage, they were strung out like a snake for nearly a mile. When we finally arrived in the car, both Russ and I stood amazed in front of the building. Instead of the traditional concrete structure, the Venmony Baptist Church was made of red brick. The concrete pillars on the front porch of the church and the parsonage gave the building an elegant look. The red teak double doors into the sanctuary gave the building a distinguished appearance. The tin roof and simple shape fit the property perfectly. I had not envisioned this outcome at all, but sometimes the Lord leaves the final vision as a surprise; a pleasant surprise!

18

This House of God

A LITTLE AFTER NOON on February 28, 2010, the dedication service for the new Venmony Baptist Church and parsonage began with Shibu and I unlocking the front doors of the sanctuary for the first time. In flooded the people, a crowds so large that over half the people who came to the dedication couldn't make it inside. A canopy had been built to cover the front yard, so the over flow crowd wouldn't have to set in the hundred degrees plus temperature outside in the sun. Inside the heat was intense, but the spirit was warm and joyful. The 'who-who' of the mission were there with the vice-president, Pastor K. J. Thomas, opening the service. There were prayers, songs, psalms, declarations, and dedication of gifts to the people of Venmony. Every church in the association gave something to the new sanctuary; like chairs, fans, clocks, a communion table, rugs, and numerous other gifts to furnish the new church and parsonage. The people of the Emmanuel Baptist Church had given the bricks, doors, windows, roof, walls, and concrete, but the final touch was added by the association and its members. It was a combination of gifts and giving both from America and India that made the new church building possible.

About an hour into the service, I had the privilege of delivering the message, "This Hallowed House." Before I preached on the value of a house of worship in a churchless place, I asked Russ to join me at the new pulpit to sing a new hymn I had written for the dedication. Using George Warren's classic music to Daniel Robert's inspiring hymn, "God of Our Fathers", we sang:

Enlarge My Coast

This house of God, a place of peace and rest.
This house of God, a haven for the best.
Like a shining flame, the 'message' to proclaim,
May God in heaven, be pleased with us the same.

This house of God, a place of constant prayer.
This house of God, a home, Oh, so rare!
Like days of old, a standard to uphold,
Oh, Spirit, come, and make thy children bold.

This house of God, a people not a place.
This house of God, a chosen, holy race.
Like a forest green, a wonder to be seen,
Christ-like, and free, their living, Oh, so clean.

This house of God, a place of soul-full praise.
This house of God, in love their voices raise.
Like an angel choir, the people never tire,
But sing their thanks, their laud, and their God's desire.

This house of God, a place we dedicate.
This house of God is where we'll congregate.
May we fulfill, Thy Word to instill?
And daily walk and do the Father's will!

It is my prayer that this simple house of worship will, until the Lord's return, function as a place of worship and be an example of the truth of this hymn!

19

The First Parsonage

AFTER MY MESSAGE, THREE felicitations were shared: Pastor P. K. Rajan on behalf of the sister-churches, Russ Coffin as representative of the Emmanuel Baptist, and P. J. Johnson, the business manager of the mission. He recognized the project engineer, the head mason, the chief carpenter, and the roofing contractor for their contribution on the construction of the church and parsonage. The church pastor, Reji Mathai, thanked everyone for their support and for coming, and Reji's father, Rev. I P. C. Mathai, another pastor in the association, had the closing prayer, and Shibu the benediction. Afterward, we moved next door to the second part of the dedication service: the parsonage.

One of the first burdens I got for the pastors and their wives of Kerala was the reality that there were no parsonages in any of the 19 churches of the mission. I know this aspect of ministry is loosing acceptance in America today, I for one have lived the last 35 years of my life in one. It has been for me a blessed part of the ministry I have had for nearly forty years. In the States now, most pastors have their own homes, as it is in India, but the difference is that most pastors and their families have to live with their parents or family away from the town they are ministering in. On my first trip to India I visited 12 of the 19 churches, and no one except for Reji lived close to their flock. Most had to travel hours, and others miles to be with their people any day of the week. Most had to take public transportation which would take hours at best to get to their mission field. Reji lived in town, but had no church, but the home he was in was borrowed both for a sanctuary and a parsonage. It was then God said to me: add a parsonage to the Venmony dream.

Enlarge My Coast

When I told Shibu to make plans for a new sanctuary in Venmony, I asked him to ask the engineer to add a parsonage on the side; it increased the cost, but it would provide a place for the pastor and his family to stay. All we had to do was walk around the corner of the sanctuary and there attached to the right side of the church was a new brick home. We entered through a porch door (my wife's idea, she says a house is not a home without a porch) into a large living room. Once again, only a few people could cramp themselves into the house where Pastor T. P. Sakhai led us in the dedication. Pastor Joy Thomas, my friend from Orissa, read Psalms 127. I again had the privilege of giving the exhortation to the new residence and the purpose of the parsonage. Shaju had the dedication prayer, and then we moved into the kitchen for the most meaningful part of the service.

It is a custom in India at the dedication of any new house to light a fire in the cook stove. There to greet us by the wood stove was Annamma, the matriarch of the Simon family, and Reji's wife who would do the honors of lighting the first fire. Pastor V. P. Joseph offered the prayer and Shibu once again gave the benediction after which Sinue started the first fire in the oven. A great cheer went up from the crowd on the outside when the smoke came out of the chimney. It was time to feast and celebrate in a typical India style. The men who had at the old church started their day of cooking had by now set up the tables that would serve over 500 people a meal. It was mid-afternoon by now when the lines began to form for a meal of rice and all the other spicy foods known to that region. I had meat to eat (John 4:31–34) nobody knew of as I wandered through the feasting crowd. I visited everybody I knew in the group, friends I had come to love and respect on my three visits to their state. I am happy to report that since that first parsonage went up 2 others have come on line with a 3rd being built in Andrah Pardesh!

20

Indian Houseboat Ride

Russ Coffin's last day in India began with a final walk-around Edayappara at sunrise. After the busy day of dedication in Venmony both Russ and I slept like a rock, but were on the streets of my favorite Kerala village by 6:30 AM. I wanted to show Russ my favorite part of town: "pineapple valley".

After walking into Edayappara center, we turned right on the Salvation Army Road (my name, few streets are named in India) and then a quick left turn. To my total amazement and utter surprise my favorite valley had been transformed in my three year absence. Instead of a deep valley filled with pineapple plants, the once fruitful vale was now filled with rubber trees; a more lucrative crop in Kerala. You could see that whoever owned the valley hadn't started taping the trees yet, but they had certainly grown to a good-size in such a short time. Disappointed, I walked Russ by the dairy farm of the two sisters I had met on my first trip to Edayappara, but once again things had changed: no cows or water buffalo and no sisters. Our only joy came with two dogs that followed us partway back to the Simon house. On the way we stopped by the orphanage to say goodbye to the kids and then onto the dairy and the new Catholic Church in Mundathanam; a sanctuary under construction when I was their in 2006 and 2007. It was nice to see it finished. Our last act was to pick up a few coconuts, so Russ could taste fresh coconut milk; which he had for breakfast. After breakfast we loaded into the Simon's car for a surprise adventure. In 2006, Shibu surprised me with a special trip to the Periyar Tiger Reserve to see wild elephants in Thekkadi. In 2007, Shibu surprised Marnie and me with a special trip to the Elephant Rescue Center at Kobanadu to play with elephants. What was going to be Russ and my surprise on the seventh wedding anniversary of Shaju and Julie Simon? All Shibu would say was we were going to 'the Venice of Kerala'!

We left Edayappara with two cars filled with people. Besides Shibu's family and Shaju's family, we had Binu and two Simon cousins along for the ride. I knew exactly where we were as we traveled north to Kottayam, and sure enough my lumberyard elephant was right where we had left him on Saturday. As we left Kottayam, we headed for the coast, an area I had never been to before. Sure enough about seven miles west of Kottayam, we came to a district of flat land crisscrossed with canals. Mile after mile we crossed broad waterways cut into the land from a large lake. Huge rice fields, miles long, on both sides of the road. I could see why Shibu called it 'the Venice of Kerala'. About an hour and a half after we left Edayappara, we turned off the main road and worked our way along a narrow, dirt lane along one of those numerous canals. About a half a mile up the canal we stopped and learned of our destination: Vembanad Lake and the Kumarakom Bird Sanctuary for a traditional Indian houseboat ride.

Shibu had booked us for a four hour 'houseboat' (kettuvallam-'kuttu' means bundle, while 'vallam' means a big boat, originally these boats were used to carry rice, but had been converted over to houseboats for the tourist trade) ride on Kerala's biggest lake to experience the inland coasts of Kerala. Kumarakom is considered Kerala's best tourist area with people from around the world traveling to its pristine waters, pleasant climate, five-star resorts, and wonderful vistas. Our kettuvallam had been motorized with all the modern amenities including a television. We had a crew of three to serve us including the boatman to drive the boat, a cook to feed us (our trip included lunch, a five course meal), and an engineer/waiter; we would need his skills, for out in the middle of the lake the engine decided to quite!

21

A Four-Hour Tour

IN THE 60S THERE was a popular television comedy called "Gilligan's Island." It had a catchy tune and song that began: "Now sit right back and I'll tell you a tale, a tale of a fateful trip that started from a tropic port aboard a tiny ship . . . five passengers set sail that day for a three-hour tour, a three-hour tour!" As we floated aimlessly waiting for our boat mechanic to fix our dead engine, I thought of Gilligan, the Skipper, the Millionaire and his Wife, the Movie Star, the Professor, and Mary Ann and their fate; would we too eventually drift onto one of the many islands in Vembanad Lake?

Our passenger list numbered eleven and our crew was three and our tour was to last four hours (noon to four). The first part of the trip had gone well as we made our way up a wide canal to the mouth of a sea-size inland lake. We couldn't make out the far shore as we crept into the open water of Vembanad Lake. Within sight were numerous other boats just like ours. Most Indian houseboats are used as floating hotel rooms. People rent them and stay on them for up to a few weeks. Once the boat leaves shore it has everything a person could want including bedrooms, entertainment centers, phones, and generators for lights at night. Normally the boats are tied up on shore during the night, and we saw countless houseboats still on shore as we traveled along the eastern edge of the lake. We also saw many fishing boats, and smaller boats carrying cargo, like hay and even one barge full of water. Along the shore there were many rice fields and many animals grazing. The breeze was cool off the water, much nicer than the hot, humid air of inland Kerala. I could see instantaneously why so many people came to Kumarakom to sail.

Enlarge My Coast

Our cruise was going well and by mid-afternoon we sat down to a typical Indian meal with a main dish of fish. Once again the spices made everything very hot; the spicy food was beyond eating for me. I did enjoy the fresh fruits and the desserts were tasty, but the best part of the trip was the lakeshore, the sea-breeze, and the lapping of the water against the hull of the boat. At times the boatman would simply turn the motor off and let us drift. I even got into the pilot's seat and guided us for a few drifts. Around four I was eating banana chips and drinking cold water watching the various species of birds flying around (we were in a bird sanctuary), when the boatman came from the back of the boat and tried to start the engine, and nothing happened.

At first we didn't notice because we were all enjoying the peace and quiet of the afternoon. My only regret was we saw no large animals on the shore, and after four hours I was getting a bit sea-sick (I don't do well on water, I love watching water and hearing water and drinking water, but four hours is to long to be on the water) with all the rocking. It was then we realized that something was amiss. I walked back to the back of the houseboat to see one of our crew in a hole under the kitchen with another member of the crew handing him some tools-"if not for the courage of the fearless crew the "Minnow" (Kochi-Rani was the name of our boat) would be lost!" Forty minutes after their first failed attempt to restart the engine, the boatman was successful and we headed back to shore. There would be no 'Gilligan's Island' adventure for us, besides Russ had to leave for Trivandrum before midnight to catch his flight home. Our India trip together was drawing to a close as we sailed the coastline of this massive body of water.

We were only about a half an hour late in landing. Our four-hour tour had taken just a bit longer than planned, but the fellowship was sweet, the cruise was refreshing, and the lake was pleasant: 'the weather was never rough, and our tiny ship was never tossed' and the experience will forever be remembered for the brotherhood, and not the breakdown!

22

Goodbye to Russ

MOSES HAD JOSHUA, DAVID had Jonathan, Peter had John, and I had Russ. It was a sad moment for me to see Russ Coffin get into Shaju's car for the long trip south to the coastal airport at Trivandrum. I was not sad because I wasn't going, for you must have figured out by now that every day I spend in India is like a day in Heaven to me. What was sad was the fact that Russ, who had also had a great time, had to leave and miss out on the great adventures left on this trip. I was alone again in India, a joy I had first experienced in 2006, but in 2006 I didn't have a traveling friend like Russ.

Russ and I were a perfect match when it came to being together and doing things together on this Indian adventure; I learned that on our first fishing trip together in 1992. I was actually surprised to see just how easily Russ adapted to the culture and customs on this his first overseas mission's trip. A homebody from Otis, Maine fit in wonderfully to everything India had to throw at him. What amazed me most was Russ had no hesitation to praying and preaching and practicing spiritual and practical duties that he had never attempted before. Russ had become an ideal companion and a helpful helper in this my third trip to the subcontinent, and his comradeship I would miss.

Around 9:30 PM, after a 9:30 AM to a 6:30 PM day experiencing an Indian houseboat ride (remember the cruise only took four an a half hours, another example just how difficult it is to travel anywhere in India), Binu, Shaju, and Russ left Shibu's house for an early morning flight out of India. Immediately after they left I called Coleen to tell her that Russ was on his way home. I know his wife Bev was concerned about him traveling alone, but as I tell everyone when I travel alone, I am never alone because the

Lord Jesus is always my co-pilot. I went to sleep that night with the full confidence that Russ would do just fine and that he was in good hands, and he was and he did!

Part of saying goodbye to someone is saying hello to someone else. Russ would make the flights home without delays or difficulties of any kind. I would hear within a couple of day that he had made the long journey back to Otis filled with tales of India. I had loaded his suitcase with articles I had already received in India, and he had the privilege of delivering these gifts. I still had two more weeks to finish my course and it was helpful for me to have Russ lighten my load. He did that in a practical way by taking some things home for me, but in another way he had already lightened my load as far as the mission trip was concerned. Now I had an ally in the debate of how much we are to help our brothers and sisters in India. Unless you have gone there it is sometimes difficult to understand the need. Russ now had a first-hand experience in the unique ministry that is the IGBC. He had seen the needs of the pastors, the churches, the college, the orphanage, and the people. Russ now could put faces to the names, and people to the ministries and that would forever remain. Hello! new representative to the mission of India!

Russ returned to his boat building job in the first week of March 2010. Russ returned to his position as husband, father, grandfather, and deacon of the Emmanuel Baptist Church. Since I have returned everybody tells me that Russ has changed, and he has. As I write this chapter over a year later after that trip, I have just returned from a trip to see my daughter in Texas and my son in North Carolina. While I was away Russ Coffin made a number of pastoral calls that he never did before when I was away from our church. I believe the flock at Emmanuel is reaping what they sowed when they send Russ with me to India; a better deacon and a new assistant pastor? Russ's coast had been enlarged!

23

A Kerala Chorus Book

I WOKE FROM ANOTHER restful Indian night's sleep not knowing what time it was. The battery in the wristwatch I brought for the trip died at 12:15 AM on March 2, 2010. As I dug out my backup (a pocket watch my dear wife had given me 37 years before), I realized that I was on my own and that the second half of my third Indian trip had begun!

Tuesday would be a quiet day for me in Edayappara. The only activity on the docket was the weekly pastor's prayer meeting at Shaju's house that evening. Having been through the busy times and slow times in Kerala before, I had come prepared with a few special projects that had been on my 'to-do' list for awhile. One of the aspects of a busy pastorate is the lack of quiet time that allows one to just focus on one task. In the church of the twenty-first century, you have to be able to multi-task which for me often brings confusion. I am at best a one function individual. I love to concentrate on one job, get it done and move on to the next task. India has always allowed me to do just that. Without the responsibilities of organization, leadership, or direction, I am free in India to, for example, write a chorus book (Ephesians 5:19 and Colossians 3:16)!

Since the early 70's I have been writing hymns. Periodically, I have come up with a new message for some old music. Taking a familiar church tune, I have adapted it to fit an occasion like the dedication hymn for the new Venmony church building. Over the years I have compiled my own hymnal that now numbers 69 songs (my last composition can be found in the prelude of this book). Raised from a baby in Sunday school and Children's church, I was taught spiritual chorus from an early age. Many of the Biblical verses I now know I first learned through a chorus, scripture put to song, like 'Behold, what manner of love the Father . . .' (I John 3:1). Some of my earliest recollections of Biblical stories came through choruses, like 'Zacchaeus was a wee little man, a wee little man was he. He climbed up in a sycamore tree for the Lord he wanted to see . . .' (Luke 19:1-10) For years I have thought of taking some of those old tunes connected with those old childhood choruses and making my own chorus book, but I never seemed to have the time or quiet reflection to do so. As I packed for India, I slipped into my 'to-do' folder the ideas I had collected over the years for my personal chorus book. I would start that chorus book on March 2, 2010.

Over the next two weeks, during my downtimes, I would write 53 choruses, and would compile a 23 chorus series just on the original "Only a Boy named David . . .", using other Biblical characters to teach my Awana kids of specific scriptural qualities taught by familiar individuals from the Bible; people like Moses, Daniel, Peter, Samson, Mary, Rhoda, and Jesus. (During Awana this past year, I was able to teach my kids the simple chorus about Jesus that went like this:

> Only a Saviour named Jesus,
> Only a little hill.
> Only a Saviour name Jesus,
> But they would beat and kill.
> Only a Saviour name Jesus,
> Only a rugged tree,
> Only a Saviour named Jesus,
> His glory they would not see.
> And one big spike went in His hand,
> And another in His feet.
> And one big spike went in His hand,
> And another in His feet.
> And He died, and He died,
> And He died, and He died,
> And He died, and He died,
> And He died.
> But "He is risen" from an angel's lip,
> And death had lost its grip!

What a blessing to hear children sing a chorus you composed.) It is my hope to have time to add to the collection as the Good Lord allows, or inspires, but those weeks in India were a wonderful blessing because of quiet times when old tunes revealed to me new truth; like this first little chorus

A Kerala Chorus Book

I wrote at the Simon's house on that quiet Tuesday in March I call "Praise The Lord", adapted from Seth Sykes classic chorus and music, "Thanks You, Lord":

> Praise the Lord for each day that comes.
> Praise the Lord for family and funds.
> Praise the Lord for living so free,
> In this great land of liberty.

24

A Dry, Thirsty Land

BEFORE MY FIRST MORNING alone in India was over, I had composed the first eight choruses in my new Kerala Chorus Book. I had also prepared two more messages in my India Sermon Series that I would share with the folks at Emmanuel after my return (as I write this chapter in my third India book, I have just finished that 37 sermon series). By noontime I was off to Annamma's for lunch (India fried chicken, a bit boney but tasty). Thinking I had my afternoon free, I was pleasantly surprised when Shibu showed up with an unexpected chance to make two treasured calls.

Our first stop would be an eleven mile run to Mukkada. It was a chance to return to one of the churches I had conducted a three day evangelistic crusade during my first visit to India. The small congregation was located high into the Kerala hills. We climbed steadily until we came to the dusty, dirt road that led to the church sanctuary on a side hill. What I remember best about the church was the new courtyard they had just finished in memory of Shibu and Shaju's father, Thakadiel, the founder of the church and mission. I had the privilege of being there at the dedication. The first thing I noticed as we drove to the front of the building was the people carrying water.

The area around Mukkada was experiencing their annual drought. Kerala is a tropical place with seasonal rains resulting in 'too much' or 'not enough'. With no means of collecting the abundance in the rainy season, Mukkada and many places like it always suffer through a season of no-rain. Water has to be trucked in at a high expense, a price that is very difficult for the people to bear. Ever since my first visit to Mukkada, I have never sung the chorus of Fanny Crosby's classic church hymn without thinking of my brothers and sisters at Mukkada Baptist Church:

> He hideth my soul in the cleft of the rock that shadows A DRY, THIRSTY LAND; He hideth my life in the depths of His love, and covers me there with His hand, and covers me there with His hand. (Psalms 63:1)

Pastor Robin and the congregation at Mukkada face untold hardships, but as with their other brethren in India they seem to trust, as the Psalmist, in the powerful hands of the Almighty. Each and every time I have visited Mukkada the topic of conversation has always been more about the water of the Word than drinking water!

Shibu had brought me to Mukkada, not to see 'the dry, thirsty land' again, but the newest purchase of the mission. Next door to the Mukkada sanctuary was an old home that had been abandoned. The mission had brought the building and land to make a parsonage for those who would be pastor at Mukkada. Shibu knew of my passion for the needs of the pastors of Kerala, whether motorcycles or homes, so he wanted me to see the latest attempt to help the local pastors live near their pastorates. Interestingly, the money for the purchase had come for the people of a church that I had pastored in the 1980s, the Calvary Baptist Church of Westfield, Maine. It was at Calvary I first meet Brother Thakadiel, and upon my first return from India was asked to share my experiences. Westfield had built one of the original IGBC church sanctuaries and I was pleased to see they still had a passion for Kerala. I had challenged them with my parsonage vision, so my smile was a bit wider as Shibu and Pastor Robin took me around the grounds and told me of their plans. Another spiritual watering hole for 'a dry, thirsty land'! Amen!!!

25

Triple B on Elephant Hill

OUR SECOND CALL OF the afternoon was to visit an old pastor I had met and come to love from my other two trips to India. Pastor PP Mathai was the pastor of the Kangazha Baptist Church (the home church of the mission, the original church of the IGBC). I was saddened to hear that the elderly pastor had had a stroke four months before and was not doing very well. I was excited to see my old friend again when Shibu invited me on his afternoon of pastoral calls (James 1:27).

From Mukkada we traveled down to Ranni where PP was living with his son and family, about 17 miles from Edayappara (Another example of just how far Mathai had to travel from his home in Ranni to pastor at Kangazha. He would often leave his family for weeks at a time living in a side room off the Kangazha Church building.). Traveling through Ranni brought back more pleasant memories of my 2006 trip. Ranni Baptist Church is still pastored by one of the most dynamic preachers in the association, in my opinion! Interestingly, Pastor Rajan lives with his family in a house located next door to Kerala Baptist Bible College. I still remember the morning I was out for a walk and came across the pastor and his family collecting water from a roadside tap. I was surprised to see him because the Sunday before I had been at his church. It was then I began to realize the tremendous obstacle these pastors faced living so far from their flocks. We passed the Ranni Church, one of the largest and youthful congregations in the group, as we made our way up Elephant Hill to see Pastor Mathai.

By the time we reached the summit of the hill, the rough terrain had taken a toll on one of the back tires of Shibu's Scorpion (an Indian car, like an English land rover). If you have read my other books, I always seem to have a chapter about Shibu's tires. Deciding to change the tire after we returned, we started to climb a twisting, ascending trail further up the hill. After about a five minute walk we arrived at a small cottage on the brow of the hill. Greeted as usual by the neighborhood kids, we were escorted into the living room of the modest dwelling. There setting on the side of his bed was PP. He recognized me immediately, grabbed my hand, and began to cry. I was surprised because PP had always been very reserved and quiet. Instantaneously I was taken back to the morning we had gone to an early Morning Prayer meeting and had our picture taken together under a rubber tree. The reason I loved that picture was the fact that PP barely came under my armpit! A wee, little man is PP, but a big man in Christ. I was stocked by what the stroke had done to him. It was very difficult to communicate, so as we shared a late afternoon snack of fruit and soda, I sat beside him on the edge of his bed and just held his hand. About half an hour later, we left after a word of prayer. I have no doubt that the next time I meet the seventy-six year old PP Mathai it will be in Heaven!

When we got back to the car we found that the spare tire was flat as well. We were stranded on Elephant Hill. So what do you do in India, call Triple A? No Triple A in India, but there is Triple B: Binu, Bijoy, and Baby. Shibu called the boys from the college to come and help us. They had to come all the way from Edayappara, and then take the two tires to a repair shop, before getting them back on and in the car. We had two and a half hours to wait (very realistic in India), so what to do. Sure enough, just down the hill was Aunt Mary (Annamma's father's sister). The elderly lady was very hospitable and entertained us with wonderful stories and more fruit! We didn't get back to Edyappara until nearly seven; just in time for the Pastor's Prayer Meeting, where I had a chance to share a message on "Dare To Be A Daniel" (Daniel 1:8); a very interesting day indeed in Kerala, but very typical as well!

26

Lost in the Mountains of Kerala

MY 15TH DAY IN India began with the typical sounds of birds singing, traffic noise, and village music. I have come to love waking up in India. It is so different than America now, but how I remember America when I was a boy coming awake to the sounds of the farm. I think that is why I love India; it takes me back to a simpler time in my life.

My morning was spent writing songs, preparing sermons, and walking over to the college to check my e-mail. I was concerned about my friend Russ and whether or not he made it back to Maine safely. Sure enough, Coleen had written and the word was Russ was on the final leg of his trip from New York to Bangor. The Lord had answered my prayer and had kept Russ safe, a responsibility I felt taken from my shoulders. As I stepped outside into a 110 degree noontime, I was met by my friend Joy Thomas. He asked were I was off to and I told him back to Shibu's. He asked if I wanted a ride on his motorcycle, and I said, "Sure?" (It was a wild ride beyond your imagination; a real white-knuckle trip including close-calls, high-speed turns, animals in the road, dodging people, and blind corners, and all that in a mile and a few minutes!) I will never do that again!!!

One of the joys of each of my trips to India had been a day visiting the mountains of eastern Kerala. It was a Wednesday, and we were going to visit two of the churches of the IGBC for their mid-week prayer meetings. Little did we know of the adventure that would await us, for it would take us twelve hours to finish the 200 mile marathon into some of the most beautiful mountains, yet, at the same time, most difficult roads I have yet to experience in my life. On the way I would be able to see one of my students from the KBBC class of 2006, Shaji Matthew, the newest pastor of the

Lost in the Mountains of Kerala

Thompilkandam Baptist Church. We also stopped at the Koch Kamakshi Baptist Church for a service with Pastor Binu and his congregation. Having visited these places once before, the road to and from was very familiar and the path unrestricted. We had a grand time with both groups, including the opportunity to meet Shaji new wife and baby Sarah. It was well into the evening when we sang the last hymn at Koch Kamakshi and headed home, but for us the adventure was just beginning.

On the way back to Edayappara, Shibu wanted to visit a pastor who had made contact with him about the possibility of joining with the association; who also happened to be the father of the current KBBC librarian. He thought it would be good to make a call; it wouldn't take us long, or so we thought. Shibu felt he knew were they lived and set Binu, our driver, on a course for their home. We left Koch at 8:30 PM but didn't find the home, just a few miles away, until 10:30 PM. I can honestly say in that two hours (especially the last four miles) we traveled on some of the roughest road I have ever experienced; retracing our travels a couple of time before we got our bearings. Eventually, we found Elappara and the home of Pastor Thank. The pastor had one year of training at KBBC before returning to his home village and starting two churches. His family owned a tea and vegetable farm which gave him his income. Despite the hour, nearly eleven, a full course meal was waiting for us. Also waiting for us was his daughter Sonya, another sister, and the mother. The meal was hot and spicy, so I spent time talking with the pastor about his farm: two acres of tea that was picked every fifteen days by three laborers the year around. They also grew coffee, cardamom, green beans, and other fresh vegetables.

When we left around mid-night, the pastor offered us the directions to a short-cut back to the main highway, and as people are often willing to do at night, we took it. However, within miles of us leaving the Thank's homestead, we were lost again in the back lanes that crisscross the mountains of eastern Kerala; our only distraction- rabbits!

27

Rabbit for Lunch

As we worked our way through the back roads and side lanes of mountainous Kerala trying to find the KK Road (Kottayam to Kumil) back to Kangazha, we were periodically assailed by mountain rabbits from the underbrush. Unknown to me, the people of Kerala love rabbit, but the creatures are now endangered so it is illegal to hunt them, but road-kill is permitted. In the blackness of a Kerala countryside, it was hard to get a glimpse of the fleet-footed animals unless they came under the glare of our headlights. Rabbit after rabbit played 'chicken' with Binu until one came to close to the front bumper. A cheer went up from those in the car when a heavy 'thump' was heard in the front of the car. Quickly, Binu stopped the car and sure enough there in front of the Scorpion was the biggest rabbit I have ever seen. I have a marvelous picture of Shibu holding up the gigantic rabbit by the side of a desolate road near a tea field with an ear to ear grin on his face. Just before Shibu put the rabbit in a bag he said one word: 'lunch'! Shortly after the 'kill', we found the KK Road which got us back home around two in the morning.

I only got about six hours sleep before I was up to officially begin the second half of my India mission. My day was filled with a number of interesting events:

1. A meeting with my good friend Pastor Johnson Matthews to get an update on his work about five miles from KBBC.
2. The official hanging of Russ's bell at Kerala Baptist Bible College. I had the privilege of ringing it for the first time; it sounded great, a grand echo.

3. A visit to the KBBC closet, a ministry our church in Ellsworth helped Julie Simon, Shibu's wife, start. It contained personal items for the students donated by the ladies of our church; like toothpaste, shampoo, soap, and towels.
4. I went over to the new land to watch the staff harvest tapioca; then back to Annamma's house to watch them cut it up, and finally to the top of the roof at Bethany School to see the staff spread the finish product out for drying.
5. A stop by the mission office to check my e-mails to which I found I had heard from my wife Coleen, my daughter Marnie, and my brother Mike.

And then there was my first ever rabbit lunch!

As true to his word from the roadside in the Kerala hills, I was invited over to Annamma's house for lunch and the menu included fresh rabbit. I had seen plenty of rabbits in Maine, and had on occasion accidental hit a rabbit or two, but had never actually eaten rabbit. I had eaten plenty of wild meat in my time, but drew the line at rabbit because of my wife's love affair with the cute creatures. Ever since our courting days, Coleen and I have seen the rabbit as an omen of blessing. Each and every time we would see one we smiled at the symbolism. As I sat down to my first rabbit meal, I knew my wife wouldn't understand, but she didn't know, and I had always wondered what they tasted like, so when in India eat what the Indians eat (with the exception of rice).

I can say that it was the best meat I have ever eaten in India. It was sweet without that wild wilderness taste that often comes with a wild animal. Some say that it tastes like chicken, but nothing like Indian chicken. It was full of favor, and I agreed with Paul as I finished the last bite:

> ...meats, which God hath created to be received with thanksgiving of them which believe and know the truth. For every creature of God is good, and nothing to be refused, if it be received with thanksgiving: for it is sanctified by the word of God and prayer. (I Timothy 4:3–5)

Rabbit is a meat that I would recommend to any that has a chance to partake; even if that rabbit is 'road-kill' from a mission trip into the mountains of eastern Kerala! Part of 'enlarging your coast' is eating something different.

28

The Two Jewels of India

MOST HAVE HEARD OF 'the jewel of India', a gigantic gem stone that is world famous. Unknown to most, there residence in Edyappara two-Julies that are rare gems indeed!

One of the joys of revisiting the boys (Shibu and Shaju) is the opportunity to visit with their wives. Each brother married a lady by the name of Julie. Rare did a day pass in India that my path didn't cross either of these two 'jewels'. I was staying with one in her home just outside town, and went to the other's home more often than not for lunch, or supper. Shibu's Julie prepared my breakfast and Shaju's Julie prepared my dinner on a daily bases. Beside meals, Shibu's Julie did my laundry. I still remember the breakfast on my 17th day when I sat at the dinning room table and was asked by Joshua, the Simon's oldest child, "Why I was wearing his father's shirt?"

My wife will tell you that of all things in this world I have the least respect for my cloths, or any cloths. I have never thought much on what I will wear or should wear, following closely Jesus admonition:

> Therefore take no thought, saying...
> Wherewithal shall we be clothed? (Matthew 6:31)

It seems as I was taking my cloths off the cloth line on the second floor balcony, I accidentally took one of Shibu's shirts for mine own. Even Joshua recognized his father's shirt and I couldn't tell the difference between mine and his. What I remembered best about the encounter was the way Julie dealt with the situation as she served me my first breakfast of broiled bananas with a side-order of Julie's world-famous English toast. Each Julie has always gone out of their way to treat me with the little extras that has made my time in Kerala so meaningful; like the lunch I had after the shirt-affair.

The Two Jewels of India

The morning quickly went by with further study (three more sermons in my India series) and song writing (six more chorus for my Kerala Chorus Book) filling my morning. Lunch at Annamma's house, where Shaju and Julie and Jerry also live, usually happened around one o'clock. I eat later so that I wouldn't have to bother either Julies with an evening meal. Two meals a day in that hot and humid climate (115 degrees that day) was enough for me. I will confess that it also got me away from having to pick through another spicy Indian dish! Knowing of my western eating habits, Shaju's Julie was always experimenting with American foods to feed me. Julie loves to cook (Shibu's Julie not as well), and saw me as a challenge to her cooking skills. Unlike Shibu's Julie, Shaju's Julie has never been to the States. All she knows about American cooking she has learned from her mother-in-law, or through trial and error. Waiting for me at Annamma's table was a baked potato, the first I had ever had in India, and a piece of fresh fish without all the spices usually added. Both were excellent, just like the lady who prepared it. Julie even had plenty of butter for my 'baker', just like I like it!

That night I had a chance to go with Shaju to the Poovanmala Baptist Church for a service where I preached on "Sitting At The Feet Of Jesus" (Luke 10:39). Pastor Thomas showed me the picture he had of him and Marnie the day she presented him with the keys to a new motorcycle that our church had purchased for him (another one of Russ's projects). On the way home that night I experienced my first ever thunder and lighting storm in India. It didn't rain much (Oh, how they needed the rain), but the light show was spectacular, as were the snakes we saw crossing the road in front of Shaju's car; another first for me. It was then Shaju told me that they had caught two king cobras (one 15 feet and the other 13 feet long) in the area; something still on my 'to-see' wish list. Driving into Shibu's yard who was there to greet me as she had done so many late nights before, one of the two jewels of India, with a late evening snack and a pleasant conversation! When I think of the Julies of India, I am reminded of this admonish from Paul:

> I commend unto you Phebe (Julie) our sister, which is a servant of the church which is at Cenchrea (Kangazha); that ye receive her in the Lord, as becometh saints, and that ye assist her in whatsoever business she hath need of you: for she hath been a succourer of many, and myself also. (Romans 16:1–2)

Just as the Julies of Edayappara have been succourers (helpers) of me on my trips to their homeland!

29

A Birthday in a Foreign Land

I will never forget my 59th birthday; the only birthday I ever celebrated in a foreign land. I have been away from home on other birthdays, but never one so far from home!

Saturday came in hot (I kept a weather record in my trip journal), but more pleasant (actually March 6, 2010 was the coolest day I experienced in my 30 days in India with the high only reaching 114) after the rain of the previous evening. There was a slight overcast as well that kept the temperature down. I slept in to eight, my first birthday present to myself. I only had one event on the mission schedule, an afternoon challenge to the youth of the Kangazha Church. They were having a volleyball tournament to get the Gospel out to the non-churched kids in the neighborhood. I was pleased to be asked to share a simple Gospel message, even if it was my birthday. What a better birthday present than to see someone born-again on your birthday, and to think their spiritual birthday would forever be my physical birthday! One of the choruses I wrote on my birthday was adapted from Arthur Woolsey's classic children's tune to 'Saved To Tell Others', which I changed to "Have They Ever Heard?"

> We're told, told to go outward
> To a world lost in sin.
> Told, told to be faithful
> To the people we would win.
> Told, told to invite them
> To believe in His Word.
> We're told, told, told by the Lord,
> But have they ever heard?

A Birthday in a Foreign Land

I based the chorus on Paul's classic exhortation in Romans 10:14–17:

> How than shall they call on Him in whom they have not believed? And how shall they believe in Him of whom they have not heard? And how shall they hear without a preacher? And how shall they preach, except they be sent? As it is written, how beautiful are the feet of them that preach the gospel of peace, and bring glad tidings of good things! But they have not all obeyed the gospel. For Isaiah saith, Lord, who hath believed our report? So then faith cometh by hearing, and hearing by the word of God.

Instead of having breakfast at Shibu and Julies, I was told that that morning I would be eating with Shaju and Julie because Joshua was having a field trip and his parents were going along. The field trip was the truth, but the breakfast was a cover story. Sure enough the Simon's left as if going on the field trip. I was left alone to walk over to Shaju's for breakfast. Little did I know what was waiting for me when I walked into the seating room at Annamma's house? The entire Simon family was waiting for me, for a surprise birthday breakfast, cake and all. It seems my wife had let the family in on my birth date, and secrets were shared. There in the middle of the table was a birthday cake with 59 candles on top. Do you know what 59 candles look like when lit? We had a small fire going until the Simon kids helped me blow them out. We shared breakfast and the cake and then the Simon's went off to Joshua's class fields trip (a water park). I returned to the Simon's house for another surprise.

I had hardly gotten into the front door when the phone rang, and who was on the other end but my daughter Marnie calling all the way from Dallas (11 ½ hours ahead of India time-nearly midnight in Texas). It was a wonderful birthday surprise. After our conversation, I walked over to the mission office to check my e-mail, and sure enough the birthday greetings continued with e-mails from my sister Sylvia, my sister Lori, my brother Mike, and my wife Coleen. On my way home I stopped by the volleyball tournament where the young people of Kangazha sang Happy Birthday to me! As I returned back to the Simon home I was singing Gaither's classic chorus:

> We (I) are (AM) so blessed by the gifts from Your hand, I can't understand why You've loved us (ME) so much. We (I) are (AM) so blessed, we (I) just can't find a way or the words that can say, Thank You Lord, for Your touch. When we're (I'M) empty You fill

Enlarge My Coast

us (ME) till we (I) overflow. When we're (I'M) hungry You feed us (ME) and cause us (ME) to know. We (I) are (AM) so blessed, take what we (I) have to bring; take it all, everything, Lord, we (I) love you so much!

Coastal birthdays are some of the best birthdays of all!

30

Fifty-Eight Colony

ONE OF THE REASONS Shibu had kept the weekend quiet was because of the difficult journey that would start on Monday to Andrah Pardesh. I had plenty of time to rest and prepare for this unknown part of my trip. I couldn't believe the climate or the culture could be any more draining than Kerala, but the unknown is just that unknown! So I enjoyed my birthday, including, going by the orphanage where the kids also sang Happy Birthday to me. As is the custom of Kerala, I gave a piece of candy to each and everyone I met that day. I also was able to go to bed early that night, one of the shortest days of the entire trip. But my eyes didn't close until I had finished reading my 31st New Testament. Ever since I was a teenager, I have carried a copy of the New Testament around in my back pocket (I now have a box filled with those old battered Bibles, a testimony of just how much of the Bible can be read in your spare time). When I have found myself with some downtime (waiting at an appointment, daily quiet times) I have read a pocket New Testament. On my 59th birthday I finished another Gideon New Testament given to me by Deacon Joe Grover (another one of the deacons of the Emmanuel Baptist Church). I had also brought along another copy (after a year or more in your back pocket they need to be retired) to begin number 32 to begin my 60th year!

Sunday morning found me and Shibu at the morning service of the Edayirikkapuzha Baptist Church with Pastor K J Thomas, the vice president and oldest pastor of the IGBC. I had visited with him and his flock in 2006, and it was such a joy to be back with these old friends and see the increase in the congregation and the improvements to their church building. The sanctuary literal hangs off a side hill and the rock staircase to the front porch is beyond description. I preached on "What Faith Can Do" based on Hebrews 11:1. The time went by quickly despite the nearly three hour service. The church is only about three miles from Edayappara, so by two in the afternoon I was back having lunch with Shaju and Julie. As we eat, Shaju started to fill me in on the epic journey we would start on Monday. He had gone there many times and had gotten sick often because of the heat? I asked how it can be hotter than Kerala, but according to Shaju it was. When I walked back to Shibu's after the noon meal and saw the temperature at 119 degrees, I thought again, how can it get any hotter?

Later that afternoon Shibu and I headed for the newest church plant of the IGBC at 58 Colony. A colony in India is an unorganized territory in the United States. It is government land that has been opened up for settlement. The Gospel Team of the mission had been meeting at 58 for a number of months and had found fertile ground. The ten-mile trek from Edayappara took us through forest areas and winding roadways to a tiny village on a boulder covered side hill were primitive concrete homes had been built. Most were simple two-room structures. One could see the poverty of the region, but they were rich in the things of the Lord. The church reminded me of John's exhortation to the believers at Smyrna:

> And unto the angel of the church in Smyrna write, these things saith the first and the last, which were dead, and is alive. I know thy works, and tribulation, and poverty, (but thou art rich) and I know the blasphemy of them which say they are Jews, and are not, but are of the synagogue of Satan. Fear none of those things, which thou shalt suffer: behold, the devil shall cast some of you in prison, that ye may be tried; and ye shall have tribulation ten days: be thou faithful unto death, and I will give thee a crown of life. He that hath an ear, let him hear what the Spirit saith unto the churches: he that overcometh shall not be hurt of the second death. (Revelation 2:8–11).

About 19 individuals from four families joined Shibu and I and the Gospel Team in a kerosene lantern service on the front porch of Manoj's home. I preached on John 3:16 in a message I call 'surveying salvation'. The singing was sweet, the testimonies were heart-felt, the prayers were meaningful, and the fellowship was hospitable. As with all India church services, some food was brought out; food I know these people couldn't spare but they did. I know now that 58 colony was God's way of preparing me for what I would experience in Andrah Pardesh; a part of the Church that is poor but rich, persecuted but free, few but faithful!

31

The Four Musketeers

BESIDES THE DEDICATION OF the Venmony sanctuary and parsonage and being graduation speaker and Bible Conference teacher, the real reason my third trip to India excited me was the chance to travel into the State of Andrah Pardesh as a missionary evangelist. I had met the leadership and pastors of the Andrah Pardesh work in 2006, and had heard for the first time the amazing history of Sake Matthews and his pioneer work in the desert of central India. Now I was going to get a chance to visit the work and share in the ministry for a week, and I was going to get to do it with my three best friends in India: Shibu Simon, Shaju Simon, and Joy Thomas. One of my treasured photographs in my church office is a picture of the four of us standing in front of Annamma's house just before our great spiritual adventure; the four musketeers of Andrah Pardesh.

We left Edayappara around ten in the morning on March 8, 2010. We had barely gotten into Partathanam (just two miles outside of Edayappara) when we stopped beside the road. I thought the boys were trying to buy me a watch (my traveling watch had stopped a few days before and the morning of the trip my backup, Coleen's pocket watch, had also stopped running), but I soon discovered the boys had left some important papers at the mission's office and one of the drivers was coming to meet us. Within minutes the mission Jeep pulled up beside us and through the windows the documents were handed over; only in India! Just outside Kottayam, we stopped again this time to purchase me a watch (I am a person that loves to know the time, any time). I bought a 400 rupee (under ten bucks) watch that would keep me on time for the rest of the trip.

The Four Musketeers

At 11:15 AM, Binu dropped us off at the huge train station in Kottayam. We were catching a train north at noon. My excitement level was at five on a scale of one to five. I had dreamed of an India train ride for years. My last train ride was in 1972 when I took a train across Australia with my cousin Bob. That trip was over 1700 miles and took us a day and a half to finish it. The train trek before us would be just less than 700 miles, but would take us nearly a day to complete. As I walked the long platform, I noticed that we had no train. It was then the boys began to inform me of the philosophy of the Indian Train System:

"We will leave a noon if it takes us all day!"

While I waited I wanted a railway map to chart out travel. I wanted to know how we went, where we went, and how long it took for us to travel from place to place. In the gift shop in the upstairs lobby Shibu found me a map; it is an important piece of memorabilia from my first Indian railroad journey (I have a similar map of the Australian railroad system and the Australia journey I took nearly forty years before) with my three valued comrades. It was then the roots for the title of this book began to emerge!

As we waited Train #6382 on platform B1, I began to notice something strange. Periodically, a passenger train would come in on another track (there were six in Kottayam) and after it left a number of men would get down on the tracks and spray them with water. At first I ignored the process, but soon my puzzlement got the best of me; I had to ask my companions what was going on. It seems that Indian trains have only one place to empty their toilets, and that is on the tracks. Out in the country far from civilization is one thing, but in a big city with countless trains coming through it is necessary to flush the waste; whereby, the need of the men with the water hoses. I wish that had been the only bit of information I really didn't need to know, but my train ride to Andrah Pardesh would be filled with questions I should have never asked! Human waste wasn't the only thing thrown out of the train, and before I was through I would be adding to the trash and waste problem that is the Indian Railway System.

32

A Train Ride in India

OUR NORTHERN BOUND TRAIN pulled into the Kottayam Station from Trivandrum just fifteen minutes behind schedule; an amazing accomplishment according to the veteran train travelers I was with! Just ten minutes later, the official start of our Andrah adventure started when old (most engines are from the British era) #6382 pulled out of the station.

Binu helped us load our eight pieces of luggage (we were allowed to carry on two piece each, luggage, packages, and boxes) onto the 4th car back from the electric engine. We were one of six first-class cars followed with about a dozen second-class cars, and I believe there were a few third-class (more about the classes later) cars in the rear? We got to our birth by way of a narrow passageway that opened to the outside of the car from both sides, and the toilet and wash room that divided the car in half. Through a closed door, we walked into a crowded sleeping car. First-class is air-conditioned, so the doors and windows are always shut. The car is divided up into eight-passenger sections, with six people on one side, and two on the other side of the walkway. When the beds are closed up there is room for three people each on the seats facing each other, while on the other side the two individuals face each other. When it is time for bed, the two top beds fold down from the wall leaving the seat as the third bed on each side. On the other side of the walkway, the second bed is already hanging from the ceiling, which allows the lower bunk to be made from a section that comes down in the middle of the two seats. The entire area for eight people is about 12 feet wide by 6 feet deep by 8 feet high. Needless to say, the smallest area I have ever shared with seven people in my life, and don't forget at least

A Train Ride in India

16 pieces of luggage were also put into this small space! There were six of these sections in our half of the rail car.

The boys allowed me a window seat so I could see the countryside as we made our way slowly up the coast of Kerala. Within an hour we were traveling through Kochi, where I had come into India on my first trip. On the way we passed Lake Vembanad where we had taken the houseboat ride. Within two hours we had already stopped four times. I was beginning to understand why train travel in India was so slow, and so crowded. With each stop the train would take on passengers, and there were scores of villages we passed along the way, and each with a strange sounding name, like, Piravam and Ernakulam. I was surprised that the boys immediately got out the lunch Annamma had fixed for them; I on the other hand was so fascinated by the sights and sounds in the train I couldn't eat. I was also amazed at the change of topography as we worked our way into central Kerala. My time in India to this point had been only in southern Kerala, a very dry and very hilly country. As we got above Lake Vembanad, I could see that this part of Kerala had a lot more water. There were more rice patties, and the land was flatter. More palm trees verse rubber trees dotted the land and the houses I saw seemed to be fancier, richer if you will.

As we swayed (yes, the train does rock sideways) our way northward, I began to learn more about the Indian Railways from a very talkative Indian that was traveling with us. I learned that India has the 4th largest rail system in the world with well over 67,000 miles in tracks. There are over seven thousand different rail stations along those tracks. That we were on just one of ten thousand trains that run daily carrying 13 million passengers a day! I was not surprised to learn that the trains are always crowded especially in third-class where there is no limit on how many can get on, as the Indian Railway System moves the masses from coast to coast!

33

Train Log

As the boys talked, usually in Malayalam, I kept track of where we were and what was happening. Because they had made this trip so many times nothing was new to them except, perhaps, the passengers they were traveling with. This was the log I kept in my trip journal; based on our stops through our first half day of travel:

1. Kochi-a whistle announces that the train will leave in five minutes. The boys warn me to listen for the whistle when I am off the train!
2. Aluva-we lose two passengers, so there are just six of us verse eight of us which makes our space more comfortable, but how long will this last?
3. Kaladi-the boys for the first time allow me to step off the train, but my bodyguard Joy is right beside me; they don't trust me!
4. Kodungallur-two hours into the trip, the brothers Simon are in their beds after their first meal for an afternoon nap. I am still excited to see what is happening.
5. Irinialakuda-our trip has slowed with stops about every fifteen minutes. It will take us a week to get to Andrah Pardesh at this rate!
6. Thrissur-3:05 PM-boy am I glad I got this map. I could never pronounce these places, but each station is well marked and so it my map.
7. Cheruthuruthi-really starting to notice the trash beside the tracks. Passengers simply go to the outside door and throw their trash on the tracks. Where is the EPA when you need them?

Train Log

We are just crossing the largest river in Kerala, the Bharathapuha. It is very low with a lot of bank showing. They are telling me this is the 'breadbasket' of Kerala.

1. Ottappalam-Shibu is up from his nap, but Shaju is still sleeping; three and a half hours into our trip.
2. Palakkad-We have made the turn eastward towards Tamil Nadu. I can see the Ghats Hill in the background; these would be the Western Ghats. The churches of the IGBC in the mountains are in the Eastern Ghats. I got off the train to get a picture of these mountains. These mountains are the reason we are traveling this route, only path through these rugged hills. A major stop, over half an hour!

It is five o'clock and we have just crossed over into Tamil Nadu. The mountains on both sides of the tracks are impressive as the sun is setting behind them.

1. Coimbatore-our first stop in Tamil Nadu. South India Baptist College is located here. Another major stop, we don't leave the station until 6:05 PM.
2. Tiruppur-first stop in the dark. The station is well-lit. Shibu gets off to buy me a bag of Lays Potato Chips. Seven hours into trip I eat the chicken sandwich Annamma sent with me with a banana and an apple (best apple of the trip), but the Lays Potato Chips tasted like home.
3. Erode-a long stop at this station so they can clean the train. Shibu took me down to the third-class cars to see the difference in travel. No births, no beds, the people are packed in like sardines; first-come first serve, some don't even have seats, just standing. A lot of beggars on the platform, the boys took me away from a man dressed up like a woman who wanted money. The train pulls out of Erode at eight. By eight-thirty, I am in bed as are the other people in our birth. I read awhile with my flashlight. I will wake in Andrah Pardesh in the morning, a new coast, and a much enlarged coast.

34

Good Morning Andrah Pardesh!

I WAS IN MY train bed from 8:30 PM to 6:30 AM. By the time I got up, the sun was up, and we had traveled northeastward from central Tamil Nadu through northeastern Tamil Nadu and into southern Andrah Pardesh. We had just entered the town of Kaapada (I never could find the place on my map, but the boys said we were only six hours from our destination), Andrah Pardesh. I woke up twice during our night journey, 12:05 and 3:35. I tossed and turned most of the night as well. The air-conditioner was actually a bit cold, so I used the sheet they provided for us. I was surprised I didn't have a backache, so overall my first night on an Indian train went better than expected. My first look out the window revealed that the mountains had been replaced with flat land for as far as you could see with sunflower fields everywhere and huge flocks of goats. My first through is that we had made a wrong turn and had ended up in Texas. I immediately knew I wasn't in the Lone Star State when I saw a man plowing with a team of oxen!

Another change I noticed immediately was the change in sound from the engine just ahead of us. Over night we had somewhere switched from an electric engine to a diesel engine. The boys said they had a good nights sleep as well. Our first stop in which we could get off the train took place in Kondapuram Station. It was here I had one of my worst experiences in India. Shortly after getting off the train to stretch my legs, I confronted a little girl of four begging on the platform. Her hair was matted and dirty; her cloths were rags at best, but, as do most four-year olds, she had the face of an angel, despite the dirt. Hand out, hand to mouth, I knew what she wanted and if that wasn't enough, her dark eyes locked onto mine. For as far as I could see I was the only white person on the platform at Kondapuram that morning. Shibu was quick to see my dilemma and said, "Walk away!" And I did, but as I did one name came to my heart "Marnie Lee." I got back on the train, but from a hidden place I watched for the next ten-minutes 'the marnie of Kondapuram'. As the crowd began to get back into the train, I watch as the little beggar left the platform for an area across the track where I saw a young man greet her, and see if she had gotten anything from the passengers. Happily, she followed the young man (a brother, a pimp, a slave master) out of sight. I knew then my ideal of Andrah Pardesh had changed, but once again the Good Lord was preparing me for horrors that lay ahead!

Our stay in Kondapuram was long because, as we discovered, it was a water stop for the engine. Our journey continued into the heart land of Andrah. Along the way we passed a 4 stack power plant out in the middle of no-man's land. It looked like a nuclear plant to me, but the boys told me they didn't have any such plants in this part of India (I still don't believe it). By eight the boys were eating breakfast, bought from vendors that periodically passed through the train. I saw nothing to eat myself, but I was filled with the interesting sights I was seeing through the train window. Twenty hours into our trip we stopped at a small station in Tadpatri. According to the boys, there were only two more stops before we arrived at the railhead of Guntakel, our train's destination. We still had many a mile to travel by car, but the train part of our trip was nearly over. On occasion, we would pass another passenger train, and some times a train hauling some kind of ore. There seemed to be a lot of construction taking place along the track? But the towns were far apart, and the landscape was flat and mostly empty. We did cross a few rivers, but again most of them were dry, some without any water at all. I thought Mukkada was 'a dry, thirsty land', but it had nothing on what I saw in my first few hours in Andrah Pardesh. My heart echoed David's feelings recorded in Psalms 63:1:

> O God, thou art my God; early will I seek Thee: my soul thirsteth for Thee, my flesh longeth for Thee IN A DRY AND THIRSTY LAND,
> where no water is.

35

Guntakel Baptist Church

TWENTY-FOUR HOURS AFTER WE left Edayappara, we stopped at the Andrah Pardesh town of Gooty. This was the ministry area of Pasad Sake, one of the sons of Sake Matthews. High on a hill just outside of town we could see a huge Hindu temple. It was then I felt I had arrived in a pagan land. Our stop was short and our final run into Guntakel only took a few minutes. My final point of interest before I disembarked was the sight of people fishing in two huge pools of water just outside Guntakel. I knew the water was shallow for there were people in the middle of the lake, but only standing in waist high water!

As we got off the train, Pasad and his brother David and our driver Shamash were waiting for us. The first thing that hit me was the hot air. (As I write this remembrance this morning, I have just gotten off the computer with my son Scott, a soldier in the United States army in Afghanistan. He told me that it was 116 and a very dry heat. I realized that I too had experienced such temperatures, not in the humidity of Kerala, but in the heat of Andrah!) Unlike Kerala, the air in Andrah Pardesh lacks moisture. It is super-hot, but super dry. We stayed around the train station while Shibu and Joy bought our return tickets. We would be back in five days to repeat our trek. The process took about an hour, and as we waited I looked around. The train station was much like Kottayam, just busier, and louder. There seemed to be more confusion, and once again I saw nobody that looked like me. I was once again in a strange and foreign land with a people speaking a strange and foreign language (telugu). Even the boys had to rely on a translator here, so it was nice to have others in the same boat I found myself in. Once the tickets were purchased, the bags and boxes we had brought were

Guntakel Baptist Church

loaded into Shamash's Scorpion, but unlike Shibu's Scorpion, this car had no air-conditioner, would that be a problem?

Our first stop was at the Guntakel Hotel to take a shower and clean up from our long train trip. The water was cool, but the best part of the layover was the monkey that came to the 4th story window. I was able to get a few pictures as long as I fed him banana chips. After each of us was able to clean up and feel a bit better, we were heading for the other side of town were a church had been started by the mission. The Guntakel Baptist Church was pastored by Pastor Rupert. Despite the fact it was a Tuesday afternoon; the church was meeting in a second floor room when we arrived around one o'clock. The pastor and his wife and three girls greeted us warmly, and it just wasn't the heat, as did the forty plus individuals singing there. They did have a few fans going, but it was hot, but again not humid, so I actually liked it. A traditional round of songs, of course, different songs than I had heard, but the people were very musical! The biggest difference I noticed at first was next to Kerala the people of Andrah sing more and pray less! They seem to love to clap their hands more than the people of Kerala, but that all familiar smile was on every face, just like Kerala.

My first message in Andrah Pardesh was 'constantly continuing' from Acts 2:42. After about an hour the service was over, much shorter than the average Kerala meeting. When the service was finished Pastor Rupert went out and got us all a bottle of Sprite, something that would be a continuing theme throughout the rest of my time in Andrah Pardesh. It was such a blessing to spend just an hour with Pastor Rupert and his people. I had broken the ice into another culture, and I knew like with the people of Kerala I was going to enjoy my time with the Church in Andrah Pardesh. I knew the blessings were just starting.

We had one more stop to make before we left Guntakel for Kanekel, our final destination; the boys had to eat. We found a second story restaurant with a lovely breeze, but I was more interested in the traffic outside than the food inside. Everywhere I looked there were bullock carts, more carts than cars; I was not in Kerala any longer, or Kansas, and the coast of Maine was nowhere to be seen!

36

The Journey to Kanekkallu

By two o'clock on March 9, 2010, we had left the restaurant in Guntakel to begin our 40 mile trip to the mother church of the Andrah Pardesh ministry at Kanekkallu (Kanekel). There were seven (Joy, Shaju, Shibu, Pasad, David, Shamash, and me) of us and all our stuff crammed in Shamash's land rover as we left the noise and smell (there seemed to be more animals than people in the town) of Guntakel, for the open country of far western Andrah. On my map I could see that we had literally crisscrossed the width of southern Andrah Pardesh, and had arrived in a small borderland area next to the State of Karnataka. Actually, one of the Sake boys (Isaac) had a church plant in Karnataka in the town of Bellary. The first memorable event of our journey to Kanekkalla was a Hindu temple shaped like a standing monkey on the outside of town. We had stopped for gas when I noticed the massive structure just a head of us. Standing at least a hundred feet in the air, the sanctuary was situated under the huge legs of this creature. It was just the first of numerous Hindu temples I would see on my travels through this corner of Andrah; I would see larger structures, but none more unique as I came to understand the grip Hinduism had on the culture and the citizens of this desert land! I was reminded of this admonition of Paul:

> For the invisible things of Him from the creation of the world are clearly seen, being understood by the things that are made, even His eternal power and Godhead; so that they are without excuse: because that, when they knew God, they glorified Him not as God, neither were thankful; but became vain in their imagination, and their foolish heart was darkened. Professing themselves to be wise, they became fools, and changed the glory of the

The Journey to Kanekkallu

uncorruptible God into an image made like corruptible man, and to birds, and fourfooted beasts, and creeping things. (Romans 1:20–23)

Like a foolish monkey, seemingly a favorite creature of those that would deny God!

The next noteworthy event was the large loads of hay we meet on the main road from Guntakel to Uravakonda. Pulled by a small tractor, these loose-hay loads often were as wide as the two lane highway. We had to get off the road to let them pass. It wasn't long before we also came across large loads of branches pulled by a team of bullock. At first the paved highway was very nice (the only difference between them and an America roadway was they were narrower, more like a single road pretending to be a two lane highway), but within a few miles they became very rough. The country we were traveling over was very flat, and it seems that during the rainy season most of the area floods breaking up the roads. It was often easier and smoother to travel off-road through the vast fields that line both sides of the road. Needless to say, the travel was slow and deliberate; picking our way through pothole after pothole, around rock-walls and built up boundaries that marked one field from another. Everything was dry and dusty and that oppressive heat was beyond description. When you put your arm out the car widow to catch a breath of air it was like putting your hand into a preheated oven at 400 degrees!

About halfway through our trip, we stopped at Gagijunda (rice soup) to check out a possible site for a pastor's school the mission is hoping to start in Andrah Pardesh. Because most of the pastors of Andrah and Orissa have never been to Bible School, Shibu is hoping to start an institute for these men to attend a few weeks a year. This corner of Andrah would be a central place for the men to meet, and he wanted me to see a two acre plot that might serve the purpose. It was a piece of flatland with water, ideal for building and available. I too had been dreaming of such a place for my India pastor friends; time will tell whether or not the funds can be raised for that Pastor's School. We also stopped at another piece of land before getting back on the main road; it was smaller and had few advantages that Gagijunda offered. Our travels took us through village after village spread out over the forty miles. Just outside each of these towns we usually came across huge flocks of sheep or goats or water buffalo. The sheep and the goats had shepherds, but the herds of water buffalo seemed to be wandering on their own!

Four hours after we left Guntakel we arrived in the town of Kanekkallu, and there to greet us was Sake Matthews and a number of the pastors of Andrah Pardesh. We had found an oasis of saints in a desert of unbelievers!

37

Ellie of Kanekel

THERE IN THE COURTYARD with a typical Indian welcome was the head of the Andrah mission, Sake Matthews. He and his co-pastors placed fresh-cut flowers around our necks, and greeted us as long-lost friends. The courtyard was hedged in with the beautiful Cuddapah Flat-Stone we had seen during our travels on the train. This stone is native to central Andrah and is a primary building material. The church structure was also typical of southern India, mostly made of concrete, but I did notice the same colorful ceiling coverings that I first saw at the new church in Venmony. Shibu told me that he had gotten the idea from his visits to Andrah. For me this was a visible symbol of the wonderful unity that had been established between the Church of Kerala and the Church of Andrah! Within a few minutes of getting into Kanekel, we had settled into the church (we would stay in the main church sanctuary for our five days in Kanekel) and had taken our first 'bucket' bath (no showers or running water or hot water, so we had to take a bath with water from a well next to the toilet and wash room). It wasn't as bad as it sounds, especially when you consider just how refreshing and rejuvenating that cold water felt in the heat of Kanekel. It also took me back to the days I use to draw water from a deep well by means of a hand-pump on the family farm in northern Maine!

I will never forget the moment as I came out of the wash room for the first time that our eyes met. There lying under a tree beside the church was a spotted, tan-colored dog. Her hair was matted and her eyes were sad. You could count her ribs; she looked starved. I tried to approach her, but she got up and left, shy or afraid, I couldn't tell? I entered the church and asked the boys about her. It was then I was told of what I would find amazing as I

Ellie of Kanekel

traveled around Kanekel. The community was over run with dogs; big dogs, little dogs, packs of dogs, but nobody owned a dog in the entire town. They were all stray dogs left to themselves to fend for themselves, dogs like the one in the courtyard of the Kanekel Baptist Church. Over the next five days I would make friends with Ellie (my name for the church dog) through the one thing she craved more than friendship: food. I would share my meals with her, and before our days together were over, we became companions. Ellie reminded me of my cat Eddie and how I had made friends with him when he was left to fend for himself. Ellie became my connection with home, and the realization of this wonderful proverb of Solomon:

> A righteous man regardeth the life of his beast ...
> (Proverbs 12:10)

And Levitical law:

> Thou shalt not muzzle the ox when he treadeth out the corn.
> (Deuteronomy 25:4)

Whether one that treads the corn, or guards the church, both deserve to be fed! That very first evening at Kanekel I realized there were others seeking another kind of feeding.

My second meeting in Andrah Pardesh took place on the first night we arrived at Kanekel. On the other side of town from where we stayed was the original building of Sake Matthew's ministry that he had begun thirty years before. When I entered the simple chapel, I knew I was in for an exciting evening with the people of the Sanjay Nagar Baptist Church. The structure could hold maybe fifty people crammed in, but 127 showed up that night. There were more people at the door and at the windows than in the sanctuary. It seemed that seventy-five percent of the people there were children, and their singing and clapping and chanting were inspiring. I gave a very simple Gospel message I called "Stepping Outside Your Comfort Zone" based on Philippians 4:13. A short invitation was given and two kids and an adult raised their hands for salvation, my first fruits in Andrah; it was just a foretaste of the draw of the Gospel in Andrah Pardesh, and how large my coast would grow!

38

Cell Phone Towers and Hindu Temples

I WOKE MY FIRST morning in Kanekel to the sound of mooing cows, roosters crowing, and dogs barking. I thought I was back on the Blackstone farm of my boyhood. I could also hear the noise of traffic passing by the front gate of the church courtyard. Located on the very busy main street of Kanekel, the church was a lighthouse to everything that was Hindu in Kanekel. The massive Hindu temple that dominated the center of town was just a few blocks away. I emerged from the front doors of the church to see Ellie under her favorite tree and the night guards (there was always someone around us day and night) getting their breakfast going near the storage building on the corner of the property. The heavy, iron gate that blocked the only entrance into the churchyard was still shut, but I could see through the thick bars the bullock carts, loaded donkeys, transport trucks, and auto cars as they passed by. It was time for me to explore this new world!

The first thing I did was ask how the boys had survived the night. Unlike Kerala, Andrah has mosquitoes. I had been warned, so I had brought along the best insect repellent in the world (Skin so Soft). I had tried to share it with my companions, but they had put their trust in three Indian, spiral, smoke sticks. I slept wonderfully; them, not so great! After hearing the terrible tales of the Kerala boys, I went outside to find Shamash washing his car. I discovered that morning that Shamash was a Moslem, and from what I would witness through the week the driver of the best vehicle in the area. I learned that Kanekel's population was about ten thousand, but I soon suspected that the animal population was four or five times larger. I also learned after I had

Cell Phone Towers and Hindu Temples

gotten myself cleaned up for the day that our wash and toilet room was the only one in town. Shibu had paid for the construction of the simple building because in Kanekel people go to the bathroom and cleanup in the open; I for one was thankful for our primitive facility, out of sight!

We had breakfast at David's house on the other side of town; we could have walked but Shamash took us everywhere. It was then I learned that I would be very restricted to where I could walk; it was simple, only in the church courtyard! I had come to a hot land, but I discovered on my second day a hostile land as well. My exploration would be limited to what I could see from Shamash's Scorpion, and what I would witness through the bars of the courtyard gate. I did venture once beyond my boundary and that was to only walk across the street in front of the church, and I was literally chased back into the compound by a man angrily yelling at me. I didn't know what he was yelling, but again, being the only white man in town, I was easily spotted and felt a general hostility by the general population, but wonderfully welcomed by my fellow-believers. One of the interesting things I noticed as I took my sole walk, and later as I traveled around the area, that near each Hindu temple was a cell phone tower. Everything in town was primitive, ancient, a hundred years old, but everybody seemed to have a cell phone.

Wherever we traveled Shibu had great reception, was able to keep in contract not only with the Sake brothers, but with the ministry in Kerala. He was always on his cell phone, in the train, in the car, or in the yard at Kanekel. I will never forget the night after a service that I saw Shibu coming up to me with his cell phone at his ear. He was talking to someone, but as usual I paid no attention (I pride myself in believing that I will be the last person in the world to own a cell phone) until Shibu handed the phone over and said:

"Your wife wants to talk to your!"

Sure enough, it was my wife Coleen calling all the way from Dallas, Texas (there to see our daughter) to Kanekel, India on a cell phone! I am still amazed in such a possibility, but for me the dangers of this advancement in technology can be just as evil as the Hindu Temple, just another way of keeping people from talking to the real God. Technology has become a god today to many; something to worship, and no more diabolical than the worship of the Hindu 'gods'. I know many would think me crazy, but I leave you with these simple questions, "How many spend more time on their cellphones than in the Word of God? Have cellphones brought us closer to each other, but further away from the Almighty?" They have certainly 'enlarged our coasts', but have they 'enlarged our hearts'?

39

Harvest Time in Andrah Pardesh

MY MORNINGS IN ANDRAH were spent with the pastors sharing with them my experiences in the pastorate. My theme was on 'Being A Good Soldier For Jesus Christ' based on Paul's challenge to Timothy in II Timothy 2:2–4. The longer I stayed with these godly men, the more I realized that they were on the frontline, a battlefield in which the forces of Satan and the forces of the Saviour were in mortal conflict over the souls of men. But unlike in America, they were winning and harvesting and they allowed me to fight with them and labor with them and what victories we saw and what a harvest! I had heard and preached for years on Christ's classic challenge, but had never experienced it for myself:

> Say not ye, There are yet four months, and then cometh harvest? Behold, I say unto you, Lift up your eyes, and look on the fields; for they are white already to harvest. And he that reapeth receiveth wages, and gathereth fruit unto life eternal: that both he that soweth and he that reapeth may rejoice together. And herein is the saying true, One soweth, and another reapeth. I sent you to reap that whereon ye bestoweth no labour: other men laboureth, and ye are entered into their labours. (John 4:35–38)

Each afternoon, after the heat of mid-day would pass, we would venture out into the surrounding villages for evangelistic services (three a day). I was thrilled with the three souls at Sanjay Nagar the night before, but little did I know what would happen when I would share the Gospel with the hungry hearts in places like Velagalavanga, Narsapuram, and Yapralla that first afternoon on the road?

Harvest Time in Andrah Pardesh

Our first service was about twenty miles from Kanekel where Pastor Obadiah (you will find many a Biblical name attached to the people of Andrah) had a small work (about 40 showed up to the meeting). The late afternoon service took place on the front porch of the pastor's house. When I had finished preaching on "The Greatest Story Ever Told" five adults and three children gave their lives to Christ. We then traveled about five more miles to Narsapuram where Pastor Gabriel ministered. Thirty-one people were packed into my first ever thatched-roofed church meeting. The simple mud building was certainly the poorest I had ever preached in. It reminded me of the churches my daughter Marnie visited in Nigeria. Despite the primitive surrounding four adults responded to the invitation after I preached on "What A Difference A Day Makes" based on II Corinthians 6:2-'today is the day of salvation'! Our last stop of the day was with Pastor John at Yapralla. It was nearly nine before we arrived after a very difficult ten mile trip from Narsapuram. We had to do a lot of off-road traveling to get there, yet 62 people were crammed into the church building when we arrived. Yapralla Baptist Church was a new concrete building with the fancy ceiling coverings. The music was lively and the people hospitable and encouraging. I preached on "Forgiven, Forgotten, Forever" and 2 adults and five children asked Jesus into their heart. In just over twenty-four hours, twenty-one people had responded to the Gospel call. I had never seen such openness to the Gospel in my nearly 40 years in the ministry!

By the time the week was done, I would preach 11 evangelistic messages in 11 associated churches in six days and would watch 54 people respond to a salvation invitation. It was the greatest harvest of souls I have witnessed in such a short time in all my years. I had done none of the planting, or watering, yet I was able, for at least once in my life, to share in the harvest of others. The fields are certainly 'white' in Andrah Pardesh, and unlike America, the laborers are there!

40

Street People of Kanekel

Despite the fact that the church compound at Kanekel was closed every evening with the shutting of the massive gate, during the daytime the gate was opened to whoever and whatever might decided to come through that one opening. This would include wandering cattle; remember, the Hindu believe the cow is sacred, so the streets are full of relatives that have reincarnated into such creatures. I watched with interest as these lost souls came through the gate, and where just as quickly herded out by the men that guarded us. Then there were the dogs that wandered in and out, only Ellie stayed, but the constant searching for food brought individual dogs and groups of dogs through the front gate. One afternoon I counted a group of nine dogs as they boldly came through the opening into the courtyard. They never appeared aggressive, but once again our attendants quickly herded them back into the street. And then there were the people!

One morning as I sat on my bed in the sanctuary writing another chorus, I heard strange music coming from the courtyard. Investigating, I found a pair of street musicians setting under the big shade tree by the supply building. When I arrived at the scene, a group of about ten men had gathered around the two. One man was playing a small drum, but the other man was playing an instrument I had never seen or heard before. The music was very Indian with it pulsating beat and repetition of words and melody. I got out my digital camera and recorded a song to share with my wife when I got home. While they were playing and performing, Shaju joined us to listen to a piece of Andrah I had yet enjoyed. Shaju told me the man was playing a harmonium, similar to our accordion. The rectangle box had keys on one side with a bellow on the opposite side. The man played the keys with one hand and pumped the air through the system with the other hand. One of the men standing listening to the music was Pastor B Paul who I later discovered was a harmonium player in the local Hindu temple before his salvation. After the two men finished their concert I gave them 100 rupees (two and a half dollars), for I could see that this was their livelihood. It was well worth the expense to hear the most beautiful sounds I had yet to experience in a place filled with so many sad sounds!

On another morning as I sat on my bed composing, a man come into the church sanctuary and asked me if I would pray with him. Surprised at first that he could speak English (I found only a hand-full of individuals in my week in Andrah Pardesh that I could communicate with in English), I immediately said yes thinking he was one of the pastors or guards. After we were through he left quietly and only then was I told that he was a street person. His pray had been concerning the funds needed to marry off his daughter. One of the great crimes in India is the system that requires a family to give a dowry. For many (the land on which the Venmony Baptist Church was built was bought only because of a father needing money to marry-off a daughter) the burden is too great and the stress is unbearable! I could hear in the tone of this man's voice a fear I will never have to experience. I learned later through Pasad that the man came regular to the church and that he would follow him up to see how he was doing. There was a question about his salvation, so that too would be addressed.

Periodically, I would walk to the front gate and just watch the people go by. Wandering souls in a desert prison with no hope except what animal they would come back as in their reincarnation. Street people wandering aimlessly as the dogs and cows they shared the streets with. Like Paul at Athens, my "spirit was stirred" (Acts 17:16)!

41

A Private Chef

BY OUR FORTH DAY in Kanekel, a well kept secret came to my attention that has since its revealing blessed my heart each and every time I think about it, as it is this morning as I set before my old laptop to record its meaning to me.

By my very nature I am a creature that fears few things. Where others will look for danger, difficulty, or disease, I rarely consider any of the above. I didn't need to watch for such things on our trip to Andrah Pardesh because there was a member of our team fretting and fearing for me; my dear friend Shibu. It seems that he was concerned that I might get sick eating the strange foods of Andrah Pardesh, or pick up something because of the way they prepare their food in Andrah. Unbeknown to me, Shibu took over the preparation of my food almost from the moment we arrived in Kanekel. I knew of Shibu's love of cooking (a joy he developed in his bachelor years in the United States while going to Dallas Theological Seminary), but I didn't know that he had become my private chef on this evangelical mission to the back corner of Andrah.

Each and every time we left the church compound in Shamash's Scorpion for David's house for breakfast, lunch, or supper I thought David's wife Esther was preparing my meals. Granted, I didn't know from meal to meal what I would have, but I found the foods filling and very good (not as spicy as Kerala). Kanekel is an oasis town surrounded by well-watered fields capable of growing just about anything, including a variety of vegetables. Driving through town, the main street was lined with vendors sells just about everything imaginable for food. And then there were the vendors that literally came door to door selling their produce or product. I had see a

A Private Chef

little of this in Kerala, but it was a common daily activity in Kanekel. I still remember the morning a man came into the courtyard with a bag. The contents seemed to be moving so I asked what was in the bag; his reply, "Your Lunch!" Sure enough he was a local fisherman, and had brought a number of Andrah Pardesh catfish to give to Shibu for the white man's lunch. The fish was a bit muddy tasting and strong in flavor, and in my opinion not cooked enough, but I eat it according to the standard of ". . . eat such things as are set before you . . ." (Luke 10:8) I discovered after that meal that Shibu took over the planning and preparing of every meal I eat after what he thought was an under-cooked meal, and possibly harmful.

Mornings I thought Shibu had gotten up early to pray in actuality he was downtown buying my daily 'bread'. When I thought he was off doing mission things, he was at David's house teaching Esther how to cook for an American (I was the first to visit the mission). I realized later how my meals changed, but at first, thought they just cooked differently in Andrah; more potatoes than rice, and plenty of vegetables without a heavy dose of spices and curry. Deep in my thoughts I think I was thinking that Annamma had come on the trip with us. Since my first trip in 2006, I had pretty much eaten American while staying at Annamma's house. The two Julies had followed their mother-in-law's example in my other trips. Now I thought Esther was just following their lead, but all along it was my dear friend Shibu; my 'angelic chef' (I Kings 19:6–7) all the time!

Something happened on our way back to Kerala that illustrates even better Shibu's concern for me. I had mentioned in passing about my love of onion rings, a product rarely seen in India. While Shibu was waiting to meet our train (more later), he hired a taxi to take him to the eating places in town to find a cook that would make me a batch of onion rings. When he got on our train he had two orders of onion rings for me. What a chef!

42

Last Bus from Rayadurg

OUR FIRST EXPEDITION INTO the surrounding communities of western Andrah Pardesh took us six hours to visit three churches and cover forty-five miles. On our second afternoon and evening into the backcountry, we had four churches on the schedule but only time for three, but we would have to travel sixty miles. After our daily rest period through the hottest time of the day, we eventually left Kanekel at 3:45 but without Shamash, who was off taking care of some family matters. Shamash had hired a local driver to take us around, but his inexperience was soon noticed.

It took us nearly an hour to travel the twenty miles to Muradi where 120 people were waiting to hear my message about "The Man Who Became A Boy", the story of the salvation of Zacchaeus (Luke 19:1–10). Pastor Samuel was a gracious host and when the invitation was given six adults and one child responded. As with our other meetings we had to hurry on because there was another group in Udayagolam 72 (72 because their are numerous villages with the same name, so they attach numbers to distinguish between the places) that was waiting to hear my message "Today Is The Day Of Salvation" based on Isaiah 55:6. I will always remember this place because it was a real street meeting. Our driver had a hard time finding the home of Pastor David, and when we finally did, we had quite a group of people following us. The service took place on the front porch of Pastor David's house. What I remember best about the meeting was the cow (in a pen next to the porch) that kept mooing for its supper throughout the service (54 people filled the porch and side street). It was dark before the meeting was over and I suspect the cow was the last thing on the pastor's mind. It was also noisy from the passing people, and the distraction was

Last Bus from Rayadurg

real. It was a rare service in Andrah in which nobody responded to the invitation for salvation. After the meeting however, the pastor mentioned that there were a number of people to the service that hadn't been to a meeting in years; he was hopeful.

Our last stop of the day was in a small village outside the major city of Rayadurg (another town on the border with Karnataka). I had been looking forward to this church service because of the pastor (B Paul). I had met this former Hindu priest on my first day in Kanekel. His testimony was inspiring and thrilling. His journey from being a musician to the Hindu gods to being a messenger to the only God was filled with danger and death. When he converted he was isolated and intimidated on a daily bases for years. He had stayed true, and he would be one of the five pastors ordained on our last day in Kanekel. One hundred and fifteen people crowded the simple chapel in Kothapally and I preached on "Heaven Is A Real Place." When it was over Heaven was rejoicing 'over one sinner that repenteth'! (Luke 15:10) An elderly lady had responded to the Gospel call, and we celebrated together the 'one' over the ninety and nine (Luke 15:7).

It was late into the evening when we headed back to Kanekel, but in order to get home we had to stop for gas in Rayadurg. Pulling into a gas station, a rare place in Andrah, I watched as a passenger bus pulled in about the same time. As Shibu put 1000 rupees worth of gas in our tank, I surveyed what they told me was the last bus from Rayadurg. It was a standard bus; similar to those you would see in the States, but what is different were the passengers. Besides those in the bus with there goats and chickens and other packages were the people on top of the bus. Buses are crowded in Kerala, but buses and autos and trucks are covered in Andrah. I marveled how they hung on, and then I remembered what had just happened at Pastor B Paul's church. Was it the last chance for that soul? Like the last bus from Rayadurg, there is always a space available at the foot of the Cross of Christ. I have sung for years these words from Ira Stanphill:

> "The cross upon which Jesus dies, is a shelter in which we can hide; and its grace so free is sufficient for me, and deep is its fountain as wide as the sea. Though millions have found Him a friend and have turned from the sins they have sinned, the Saviour still waits to open the gates and welcome *a sinner* before it's too late. The hand of the Saviour is strong, and the love of the Saviour is long; through sunshine or rain, through loss or in gain, the blood flows from Calvary to cleanse every stain. There's room at the Cross for you, there's room at the Cross for you; though millions have come, there's still room for *one*. Yes, there's room at the Cross for you!"

43

The Boys of Orissa

I HAD FOUGHT MOSQUITOES (Andrah Pardesh mosquitoes are smaller than our Maine mosquitoes) all night. My Skin so Soft had kept them from biting me, but their buzzing was annoying. Top that off with Joy turning the fan off because he thought it was cold (I told him the next morning there is 'no cold in India'), and I had no noise to distract me from the insect sound. I sleep with a noise every night, so without the fan to cover up the buzzing I was at the mercy of the mosquitoes.

I woke with the news that the boys from Orissa had arrived in Guntakel. It had taken them the same time to come half the distance (24 hours to cover a little over three hundred miles) we had covered in our journey to Kanekel. They would arrive at Kanekel before lunch. As I waited to greet my friends, I had a chance to talk to Pasad about the work. One of the amazing facts I learned that in all the towns I had visited or would visit theirs was the only Gospel church. Even the 'christian cults' haven't found southwestern Andrah Pardesh yet! His observation of the situation in Andrah reminded me of this challenge from Paul:

> How then shall they call on Him in whom they have not believed? And how shall they believe in Him of whom they have not heard? And how shall they hear without a preacher? And how shall they preach, except they be sent? As it is written, How beautiful are the feet of them that preach the gospel of peace, and bring glad tidings of good things. (Romans 10:14–15)

Some of the most beautiful feet I have seen in the world belong to the men of Kerala, Tamil Nadu, Andrah Pardesh, Karnataka, and Orissa!

The Boys of Orissa

Before the 'boys' arrived, I wrote my 50th chorus and my 8th hymn. I finished my 36th sermon (how about this title "Grazers, Gazers, and Gators", inspired from the surrounding scenery of Kanekel) in my India series. Then I was in the presence of nine of my spiritual champions, men of God few know but for me examples of the true believer in Christ. Ranjan Digal was the first I embraced, my walking companion from 2006 (we literally walked around Edayappara in our week together because Shibu wouldn't let me go anywhere without someone, so Ranjan became my partner). His first question, "Where is Marnie?" He had gotten to know Marnie in 2008, and as others on this journey, and thought Marnie would be accompanying me on this "journey" as well. Next to Ranjan was his father Noah, one of the senior pastors of Orissa. Also there was Samson Digal who I had first met in 2006. Then there were six men that I hadn't met before: Darserth, Surendra, Ugrisin, Sanodo, Khruso, and John. I had heard about Pastor John from Shibu; a converted policeman and now one of the great preachers and evangelists of Orissa. John and Ranjan were the only members of the team that I could directly communicate with without Joy Thomas' help.

Our first afternoon together I was able to share with them a message entitled "Is Jesus Worth Dying for"? based on Jesus' teaching found in Matthew 10:39. I can honestly say they are the only group I have ever preached to who I believed could actually die for their faith. I have preached on the possibility of martyrdom in America, but have never seriously considered that anyone of my congregation would have to lay down his life for the cause of Christ. Knowing what I knew about these men and what they had faced in the last few years, I serious wondered if I was sharing with them something that might take place in the near future for them. When I finished, they understood my challenge and simply replied:

"God's Will!"

> They reminded me of the attitude of Paul on the road to Jerusalem then he said this to those who feared for his life, "...for I am ready not to be bound only, but also to die at Jerusalem for the name of the Lord Jesus." (Acts 21:13)

Sometimes the 'coasts' of God's calling can be very dangerous shores!

44

Tears under the Trees

ONE OF THE REASONS that I was so excited to travel to Andrah Pardesh was to meet again my brother-pastors from Orissa. Shibu had told me that while we were staying at Kanekel that the boys from Orissa would be traveling from their homes to be apart of the week of activities in Andrah. Sure enough, after we had returned from our second day of meeting in Muradi (Pastor Samuel), Udayagolam (Pastor David), and Kothapally (Pastor B. Paul), where we saw another eight people saved, the pastors of Orissa were at Kanekel to greet us. Everybody had arrived safely except for one of the pastor who had gotten off the train at a scheduled stopped, but had not paid attention to the whistle and was left behind. Shibu made a point of reminded me of his warning on our way to Andrah. He knows well my adventurous feet and he didn't want me to make the same mistake the Orissa pastor had made on our trip back to Kerala!

Despite the fact that most of the Orissa pastor's can't speak English, our reunion was sweet. My friend from 2006, Ranjan, was there with his father Noah. We immediately struck up again our friendship. He got me caught up on the trials and tribulations they had been through since we had last talked face to face. Orissa had experienced dangerous persecution in 2008 (I have chronicled that persecution in a book I call "Orissa Is Burning!"), and I wanted to get a firsthand account of what had happened. It was troubling to hear of the churches that had been burned and the Christians that had been martyred, but in the aftermath, the Good Lord had relocated the survivors to other area and the Orissa Church was once again thriving. The twenty local assembles that had been scattered had started up new churches in new villages. The more Ranjan talked the more I thought of

Tears under the Trees

how the Lord had done the same thing to the Church at Jerusalem (Acts 8:1, 11:19–22). Christ's Church will go on no matter the opposition or persecution!

Some of the sweetest times I had in the courtyard of the Kanekel church were under the shade trees planted along the sides of the property. There is one thing you immediately learn in India and that is any shade is better than no shade at all. You are always looking for any shade that will get you out from under the oppressive glare of the sun. During our down times, we would often head for the shade trees because there you might also find a bit of breeze. I still remember the noontime meeting I had with the Orissa Boys and Joy Thomas. Joy wanted me to hear the testimonies of these pastors and what happened to them during 'the great trial of 2008'. He translated as each of the eight pastors shared there stories, and I am not ashamed to tell you the tears began to flow under those trees. I heard of one pastor who lost his sister in the violence. Another told of the burning of his family home and having to flee to the forest with his children and wife to survive. Noah told the story of how he was being chased by a mob that wanted him dead and how a Hindu family had taken him in and saved his life. As each relived the horror some tears came to some eyes, and I could see that there was still some deep sorrow, yet one thing I never saw or heard: bitterness or anger. Despite the killings and destruction of their life's work, their love for the people who did the damage was still there. They had already forgiven their foes, and their prayers were not for revenge but repentance! They were certainly living the teaching of Christ:

> Ye have heard that it hath been said, Thou shalt love thy neighbor, and hate thine enemy. But I say unto you, Love your enemy, bless them that curse you, do good to them that hate you, and pray for them which despitefully use you, and persecute you; that ye may be the children of your Father which is in Heaven: for He maketh His sun to rise on the evil and on the good, and sendeth rain on the just and the unjust. For if ye love them which love you, what reward have ye? Do not even the publicans the same? And if ye salute your brethren only, what do ye more than others? Do not even the publicans so? Be ye therefore perfect, even as your Father which is in heaven is perfect.
> (Matthew 5:43–48)

Under the shade trees of the Kanekel Baptist Church, I witnessed the love of Christ in full-godliness. I heard the forgiveness of Christ falling off the lips of men who had every right to be angry and hateful, yet had turned a bitter experience into a blessing. The joy in the tone of their voices and the praise in the theme of their stories made me ask if I could feel such love if it happened to me and mine. The grace of Christ was on each face. I witnessed perfection in such a manner as I have never seen it before!

45

Bullock Cart Driver for Christ

OUR THIRD AND FINAL day traveling to the sister churches of Kanekel took us to three more assemblies in the association. We only covered thirty miles, but it took us six hours to complete the mission because two miles of that trip we rode in a bullock cart!

We headed out into the heat and dust near mid-afternoon on Friday March 12, 2010. Our first stop was at Garudachedu and the pastorate of David Durham. Fifteen miles from Kanekel, this small village was surrounded by thorn bushes and the compound of mud huts was similar to what we had seen before. The simple thatched roofed sanctuary was alive with people both inside and outside as Shamash drove us to the front door (the only door in the baked-mud building). The people were already singing and the church was surrounded by smiling brown-faces. One hundred and twenty-three people gathered for our late afternoon service, but only about fifty could actually squeeze into the one room. As I sat in one of the few chairs in the sanctuary, I imagined the roof being broken up and the palsy man being lowered to the feet of Jesus by his four friends (Mark 2:1–12); that is how Biblical the structure seemed in comparison to the house in Capernaum.

The service began with a group of five small girls singing to us a series of children's songs. My daydreaming was soon interrupted by a familiar tune. Sure enough, the five young ladies were singing one of my favorite childhood choruses, "Only a Boy Named David." They of course were singing it in Telugu, the main language of Andrah Pardesh, but I sang along in English as they added the motions to this Biblical chorus. When they were done I asked the pastor if I might repeat the song in English. The smiles on the people's faces were priceless when they realized what I was singing and our bound was only strengthened. After more singing and more praying, I preached on 'The Gift of God' based on Paul's classic statement in Romans 6:23. When the service was over, Shibu gave the invitation and one elderly lady gave her heart to the Lord. All I could think of was Jesus' words to the palsy man, "Thy sins be forgiven thee"! (Mark 2:5), and like the palsy man who 'arose…and went forth' (Mark 2:12) as a healed person with a new life, so did this new sister in Christ! (II Corinthians 5:17)

Earlier that day Shibu told me that I was in for a wonderful surprise before the day was through; something he had been planning since we had arrived in Kanekel. Our travel up to this point in time in Andrah had been in Shamash's car, but our trip to our next church meeting, just two miles away, would be by other means. There waiting for us as we exited the Garudachedu Baptist Church was a bullock cart. We were to travel to Thumbiganoor by means of this traditional form of transportation, and I was going to be the bullock cart driver! What a thrill! Shibu had made arrangements with one of the believers at Garudachedu to make available his bullock cart to transport our team of five to our next church meeting. I had mentioned to Shibu that after riding an elephant in my other trips to India to ride in a bullock cart would be marvelous. Sure enough, it was all I imagined it to be, and to my surprise I would have the reins in my hand.

As we left the church area, a crowd began to gather beside the streets as we worked our way out of town. I suspect that nobody had seen a white man driving a bullock cart before. I was a novelty to say the least as I handled the two bullocks through the narrow streets of Garudachedu. My first observation was that bullocks are very slow. It took us ten minutes to get out of town and another half hour to get to Thumbiganoor, and actually we didn't make it all the way just to the crossroad leading into Thumbiganoor. Paul had taught that in the ministry of the Gospel we are to be "… all things to all men …" (I Corinthians 9:20–23) that we may by all means "save some"! That includes being a bullock cart driver for Christ!

46

Other Jobs, but One Passion!

BEFORE I EVER ARRIVED in Andrah Pardesh, I had been taught about 'and others' (Hebrews 11:35–36) by Vance Havner. I had read, studied, preached , and taught on Hebrews 11 for years, but had failed to see the change in the chapter until Vance pointed out to me in one of his books the contrast between the faithful of verses 1–35 and the faithful of verses 35–40. The first group of faithful saw great miracles (dead raised) while the 'others' only saw misery (cruel mockings and scourgings). The first group are mostly named (by faith Abraham) while the 'others' remained unnamed (they). The first group experienced blessings (quenched the violence of fire) beyond description while these 'others' only experienced some kind of bitterness (wandered about in sheepskins and goatskins). I finally saw for the first time that the hall of fame of the faithful contains two distinct groups: the blessed ones that were faithful in good times (out of weakness were made strong) and the honored ones that were faithful in bad times (being destitute, afflicted, tormented). As I rode a bullock cart from Garudachedu to Thumbiganoor, I learned of another set of 'others' I had come to know and respect!

I had been ignorant of the fact that all the pastors in Andrah Pardesh, except for Sake Matthew and his sons had other jobs besides pastoring. It was on the back of a bullock cart that I learned that some pastors were just common day laborers, like Ranjino. I had first met this man in Kerala in 2006. He stood out in the crowd of pastors (over 30 came to Kerala that year) from Andrah because he was 'a head and a shoulder' (I Samuel 9:2) taller than the other pastors. I had seen him a number of times since coming to Kanekel where I learned that he was one of the pastors our AWANA kids had bought a bicycle for. Between 2007 and 2010 our church youth ministry had been buying bicycles (21) for the pastors of Andrah, and one of my joys on this trip was to meet these pastors and see their new bikes. There was as much joy in their voices as there was in the voices of the Kerala pastors that we had bought motorcycles for. Another reason Ranjino stood out to me is the fact that he looked exactly like a man at Emmanuel Baptist. They say that everybody has a double somewhere in the world, well Ranjino and Gary could be brothers, except for the color of their skin!

As we slowly made our way through the fields between Garudachedu and Thumbiganoor, I learned that other pastors of the association were tailors, bike repairmen, masons, and bullock cart drivers. I had for the first six years of my ministry had another job besides pastoring. I had been a chicken cutter (I use to cut chickens for Kentucky Fried Chicken), a truck driver, a farm hand, and a substitute teacher at different times. Perhaps, that is why I had been able to relate so well with men like Pastor David Rag of the Thumbiganoor Baptist Church. Our meeting at his church actually took place in the church courtyard. The church building was even smaller than the others, so the 47 people that gathered sat on tarps next to the church. I preached on the healing of the leper in Matthew 8:1–3 and how we can get healing from our leprosy of sin. There were no responses to the invitation, but the shared experiences and the understanding of 'others' helped me realized just how similar our paths to the pastorate had been!

Our last stop of the day was in Malyam; about five miles from Thumbiganoor. We took the car because darkness had fallen once again on Andrah. Pastor Ezra and a large crowd (155) were waiting for us when we arrived. Once again most of the people had to stand in the doorways and windows as I preached on "No Other Name" from Acts 4:13. We ended the day rejoicing over two more people coming to Christ, why we labor on; whether the 'others' of Andrah or the 'others' of America! In this world I have been of the privileged group of faithful who have been blessed with so much 'good', while the 'others' of India have been laboring faithfully in 'bad' times. I know that when Heaven comes we will be honored together just as Paul wrote:

> God having provided some better thing for us, that they without us should not be made perfect. (Hebrews 11:40)

47

Just the Ordinary

OUR FIRST DAY IN Kanekel had taken us south to three churches of the association; three primitive sanctuaries at best. Our second day in Kanekel had taken us east and three more churches of questionable value. Our third day in Kanekel had taken us to three more assembles to the north, more mud and straw structures. In ten (the 10th was the original church of the mission) different churches I had preached to 838 people and had seen 33 of them come to Christ. My last full day in Kanekel would see those numbers rise (457 more people with 17 more salvations) as I shared messages at a youth gathering at Kanekel, another get-together with the Orissa pastors, and the keynote address to the annual convention of the Andrah Pardesh association of churches.

Saturday began as had the other days in Kanekel. The sound of the rooster woke me, and the cold water from the well shocked me back to life. This day would be different because we had to clear our bedroom for the youth rally that would start in a few hours. Fourteen of us had called the sanctuary at Kanekel Baptist our home, but for this day and the day to follow the room would be a church again. I quickly picked my things up and set them aside, so I could get to my granite desk. Each morning I had found a quiet place on the front steps of the church. Before I could settle in a couple of girls came by asking for prayer. They wanted to come to the youth rally, but today was exam day for many of the older students. They would miss the meeting, but wanted me to pray for their test!

As I got my Bible and writing materials around me (I used the chairs and the stone steps), I watched the Orissa boys having breakfast across the courtyard. Ellie was under her tree sleeping, and the busy Kanekel traffic

Enlarge My Coast

was passing in front of the gate. It was then I prepared my last message (#37) in my India Series. It would be the signature sermon in the series based on the major spiritual observation of this trip:

God's use of the ordinary to do His work.

Based on I Corinthians 1:26-28, I recalled the numerous times I had witnessed the ordinary of Andrah and Kerala, then I remembered:

God using SPIT as a healing agent—John 9:6; God using a STONE as a giant killer—I Samuel 17:49; God using a STICK as a power rod—Exodus 4:20; God using a SKRONGER (raven) as a waiter—I Kings 17:6; God using a SHOWER as a weapon—Judges 5:20; God using a SNACK to feed a multitude—John 6:9, and God using a STITCH as a ministry—Acts 9:39!

There are only ordinary things in Andrah; I saw no 'wise men', 'mighty' men, 'noble' men; I saw only 'foolish things', 'weak things', 'base things', and 'despised things', the very things God loves to use to 'confound' the world. Why?

> That no flesh should glory in His presence!
> (I Corinthians 1:29)

Sub-standard building or no buildings at all are the norm in Andrah, yet I saw more salvations in those buildings than I have seen in our up-to-code structures in America. Uneducated pastors, yet as the Sanhedrin said of Peter and John "and perceived that they were unlearned and ignorant men, they marveled; and they took knowledge of them, that they had been with Jesus." (Acts 4:13) I might have the education and the knowledge, but they are getting the souls! Poor, impoverished, yet rich (Revelation 2:9) in the things of God; "poor yet making many rich" (II Corinthians 6:10) through the Gospel of Jesus Christ! I saw what Paul described "as sorrowful, yet always rejoicing . . . as having nothing, and yet possessing all things." (II Corinthians 6:10) What I saw were ordinary people doing extraordinary things; just the ordinary yet extraordinary to God because they believed "God forbid that I should glory save in the cross . . ." (Galatians 6:14)

Oh, that 'ordinary' would come to the coast I now minister on!

48

Youth Rally at Kanekel

ONE OF THE GRAND joys of visiting India has been the privilege of meeting with the next generation that will one day be the pastors, evangelists, missionaries, pastor wives, Bible teachers, and laymen and women of the India Church. Starting with my love of the orphanage kids in Edayappara and then the college kids of Kerala Baptist Bible College and then the young people of the Kangazha Church, the kids of Kanekel and the surrounding communities only verified my belief that the Church in India will be in fine hands if the Lord should tarry. I had feared for years the fate of the church because of the lack of interest in the next generation of believers. It wasn't until I started to visit my daughter during her days at Lancaster Bible College and Dallas Theological Seminary and India that I began to meet a group of young people sold-out for Christ. Over the last ten years I have meet Marnie's companions in the desire to see the Church grow and go-on!

At eleven, the youth meeting got underway. There were 32 teenagers (the numbers were down according to their youth leaders because of the standardize school test being given that day) and nearly a dozen youth leaders in attendance. The first two hours were taken up with Biblical activities (like acting out a Bible story), Bible drills, and plenty of singing. There were testimonies and plenty of praying. Sake Matthews welcomed the group to the church. I did recognized a few of the young people from some of the churches I had preached at that week, and even a few of the students of Kerala Baptist Bible College who were home after their academic year had finished (wealth, king of truth, and father of moon-the meaning of some of their names).

Around one in the afternoon, I was introduced. My challenge to the young people was based on this exhortation to Timothy by Paul:

> Let no man despise thy youth; but be thou an example
> of the believers ... (I Timothy 4:12)

I went on to share the six characteristics of a believer as given by Paul and Biblical examples of each quality:

"in word" I used Timothy himself (II Timothy 3:15–17); "in conversation" or behavior I used Daniel (Daniel 1:8); "in charity" I used the little maid of II Kings 5 and the story of Naaman; "in spirit" I used David and his fight against the giant Goliath (I Samuel 17); "in faith" I used Isaac and the part he played in the dramatic trial on Mount Moriah (Hebrews 11:17–19), and "in purity" I used Joseph and his stand against the evil of Potiphar's wife (Genesis 39:7–23).

I admonished and exhorted them to follow these examples in their lives, for even in their 'youth' they could be examples of the believers.

I preached for about an hour and a half (remember with translation that is only about 45 minutes) then we were off for lunch. I was taken over to David's house were Esther had fried chicken, fried potatoes, and rice chips (the only good thing about rice in India). As had been my custom since Tuesday, I saved part of my meal for Ellie. I learned that she would only eat meat and rice, so I always shared. She was waiting for me when Shamash brought me back. The kids had already started their service up again, and I got a chance to set in on the finally minutes of prayer and rededication. When everything was over the kids helped set up for the big meeting that would take place that evening. The church would be too small for the gathering so a huge tent was hung in the courtyard. I was impressed with the work ethic of these kids. Besides helping the men put up the tent and set up the chairs, some of the kids started helping the cook prepare the food for the feast that would follow (they were preparing for over 500). Most of the food had to be hand-cut and prepared, a big chore, but even in India 'many hands make light work'!

49

Portrait of the Persecuted

ONLY AFTER I MEET the persecuted pastors of Orissa did I come to an understanding what Jesus meant when He said:

> Blessed are they which are persecuted for righteousness' sake: for theirs is the kingdom of heaven. Blessed are ye, when men shall revile you, and persecute you, and say all manner of evil against you falsely, for my sake. Rejoice, and be exceeding glad: for great is your reward in heaven: for so persecuted they the prophets which were before you. (Matthew 5:10–12)

On my last full day in Kanekel, I had a chance to meet one more time with my Orissa brethren, but this last time I was determined to know more of these persecuted believers.

After I spoke to the group of ten on 'ye should earnestly contend for the faith' (Jude 3), I felt it was I who should have been preached too. I had asked Joy if I might hear the testimonies of the men, and what I heard put me to shame. Despite over 40 years in direct Christian ministry, I have accomplished little despite having so much; while they have accomplish much having so little. Here is the summary of what I heard that afternoon under the shade tree beside the Kanekel Baptist Church:

1. Joy-42 years old, but only 13 years in Christ, yet he had already been a missionary to three states in India, and now as the director of the Orissa ministry had planted over twenty church; seen those churches destroyed through persecution, yet has started a dozen more in other areas of Orissa.

Enlarge My Coast

2. Ranjan-31 years old, but 14 years in Christ, the youngest of the group but a daring evangelist who shortly after the persecution held youth rallies despite the danger.
3. Noah-50 years old, but 25 years in Christ, Ranjan's father and one of the senior pastors; his life was on the line many times during the persecution, but the Good Lord saved him to reorganize and restart the scattered churches.
4. Samson-50 years old and also 25 years in Christ suffered the martyrdom of a sister and brother-in-law in the conflict, yet I heard no bitterness or hatred in his voice as he told of the lose his family suffered.
5. John-60 years old and 55 years in the faith, the oldest Christian of the group with his salvation at five when missionaries from England came to his village; he spend the bulk of his life as a police officer, but when the persecution happened he retired to give the rest of his life to the Gospel.
6. Darserth-50 years old, but only 8 years in the faith, a former member of the Hindu faith now a pastor and preacher of the Good News of Jesus Christ.
7. Surendra-65 years old and 21 years in Christ, the senior member of the Orissa pastors and faithful preacher into old age (most Indian men live short lives).
8. Sanodo-45 years old and 15 years in the faith, the quiet member of the team, but a constant voice of evangelism and encouragement to the persecuted church.
9. Khruso-60 years old, but 30 years in the faith, I was impressed with his Bible and the years of wear I saw in its pages, a fitting testimony to the place God's Word plays in the strength of faith of these persecuted pastors.
10. Ugrisin-52 years old and 25 years in the faith, another pastor I had just met but well versed in the Bible and a champion for Christ in Orissa.

They closed our gathering by singing a 'thanksgiving' song in Cuie, their native tongue:
"Rejoice, and be exceeding glad….." is how these men live their lives!

50

David, Rupert, and John Kennedy

I SPENT THE REST of my afternoon watching the labor it takes to put on a meal for 500 people in Andrah. As I wandered around the courtyard of the Kanekel church, Ellie followed me much like my cat Eddie follows me at home. I know like Eddie, Ellie was looking to me to get her a few bits of the food being prepared. After five days, I had trained her to recognize that I was a meal ticket. The 'boys' were surprised that I had been able in such a short time to get Ellie to trust me, as with the people of Andrah.

Another joy that afternoon was the arrival of the pastors and people from the surrounding towns for their annual convention. Now familiar faces began to appear as the crowd grew into the early evening. Perhaps, the most amazing appearance was the pastor from the Guntakel Church, Pastor Rupert. I saw him as he drove into the courtyard on his motorcycle, but he wasn't alone. There on the back of his small bike were two other men, and each of them was carrying a bag or two. Rupert had his bags on his lap and on the handlebars of the motorcycle. You could hardly see the bike for the passengers and the packages. Once again I stood in amazement at the ability of the Indian people to get around on small vehicles with the maximum amount of passengers. Even as I write this chapter, in my mind's eye I see the autos, the motorcycles, the buses, and the cars filled to capacity in Kerala, but in Andrah Pardesh the people seemed to step it up a notch, as in the case of David, Rupert, and John Kennedy.

Yes, John Kennedy! Rupert saw me immediately and came over to introduce two of the men from his church that I didn't get to see on my first visit because they were working the afternoon of our service together. They wanted to met me and come to the convention, so to save money they traveled the 40 miles by bike. I couldn't pass up asking how John Kennedy got his name, and sure enough he was named after our assassinated president. Born in 1965, two years after Kennedy's death, the news of the murder had reached Guntakel and John's parents honored the memory of our president by naming their son after him. Another example of just how popular Kennedy was, not only in America, but in the uttermost places of this planet. I marveled how they had made the trip from Guntakel to Kanekel together on a motorcycle, and their simple reply was that they did it all the time. The adaptability of the Indian people is something that mystifies and challenges me to this day!

That evening I joined with David, Rupert, John Kennedy and 412 other people in a time of celebration for the glorious year that had passed. I preached on "The Great Commission" of Matthew 28:19, and saw the fruits of the great commission as fifteen more people responded to the invitation, the most in one service. I had few words except 'to God be the glory' for in five short days fifty people had accepted Christ as Saviour. Pastors like Rupert would have new members to bring "up in the nurture and admonition of the Lord." (Ephesians 6:4) Before each trip to India, I have always printed a set of desires (Psalms 37:4) in the back of my trip journal. One of those desires for 2010 was "to see more people saved on this trip than my other two trips combined." In my two previous trips I had the privilege to see eight people come to know the Lord. I still had four days left and the grace of God would give me nearly seven times that number. As the congregation feasted after the service, I didn't need any food because I was already full of the harvest of souls the Lord had given me in and around Kanekel. As I watched Ellie picking up the leftovers, I was left with the soul-satisfaction of God's answer to my prayer! What an amazing God we serve; what a mighty God we serve! I began to sing another favorite chorus by Keith Phillips:

> What a mighty God we serve.
> What a mighty God we serve.
> Angels bow before Him;
> Heaven and earth adore Him;
> What a mighty God we serve!

He had certainly done many great and mighty things in this 'enlarged coast'.

51

Ordination Sunday

THE LORD WAS SHATTERING all kind of records in my side trip to Andrah Pardesh in 2010. I still remember my first trip to the Miramichi River with my father-in-law in 1991. We had been fishing the mighty Atlantic salmon together since 1979 in Maine. Over those 12 years I had caught only 23 of these elusive fish, but in my first three days in Canada I landed 27. I was having a similar spiritual fishing trip in Andrah, but an even greater statistic would be smashed on my last day in Kanekel. Since my own ordination into the pastorate in 1979, I have had the privilege to set in on five ordination counsels. Five men I examined with others and gave approval with others to a public ordination service. One day in March 2010, I would double that number!

Since the beginning of the mission in Andrah Pardesh thirty years before, only Sake Matthews had ever been ordained. Over the few years the mission and the IGBC had been working together, Shibu had encouraged the leadership of the mission to make it priority to start ordaining the men that were leading the area churches. Standards were set and lives were examined over those years and it would be on Sunday, March 14, 2010 that the first group of pastors would be ordained in a public gathering of the Andrah churches. I had the honor of setting in on one of the counsel meetings the day before, and was given the honor of preaching the keynote address to the men being ordained. Over seven hundred people gathered in the courtyard of the Kanekel Church to witness this first in the history of the ministry of the Andrah Pardesh Churches as Pastor Pasad of the Gooty Church, Pastor Isaac of the Bellary Church, Pastor Ezra of the Malyam Church, Pastor Paul of the Kothapally Church, and Pastor John of the Yapralla Church were ordained publicly into the service of the Lord Jesus Christ.

The three hour and fifteen minute service included lots of singing and even more praying before Shibu and Shaju and I sang 'To God Be The Glory Great Things He Had Done"; a first for us that we would repeat in my farewell service at Kangazha Church two days later. Everybody thought we made a good trio! There were more speeches and testimonies before I had a chance to share my message on "Fabulous Fables" based on II Timothy 4:3-4 and the dangers facing the modern pastor. There was the tradition of the 'laying on of hands' and the Simon boys presented to each of the new reverends a new Bible in the Telugu language. There was an invitation given as well and four more names were written down in the Lamb's book of Life (Revelation 21:27). Fifty-four souls in six days! I lead my first person to Christ in a nursing home in Athens, Georgia in 1970, I didn't lead my fifty-fourth person to Christ until 1976: six days verses six years!

The last few minutes of this special service was not directed to the five honored and honorable men, but for the four musketeers from Kerala. As with all departures in India, there is a formal farewell. We would be leaving Kanekel for Guntakel in a couple of hours, so a few more Kanekel flowers had to die. Each of us got a gorgeous string of flowers for our necks (how I wished Coleen could have had them, their smell was divine) and a traditional Andrah Pardesh shawl. Unknown to me, this cloth covering isn't just for women. Used for warmth in Andrah on those rare cool days, it is the Andrah symbol for friendship. The four of us stood before the crowd with a heavy covering of flowers only to be added to a light cotton shawl. Have you forgotten it was over 100 degrees, though the expression was much appreciated, it got unpleasant quite quickly in the heat? Following the ceremony another feast, but once again I preferred to feed Ellie her last meal because once again I was already full and feasting on the marvelous spiritual meals I had already been feed in Andrah Pardesh; again "I have (had) meat to eat that ye (they) know (knew) not off." (John 4:32)

52

And Then There Were Three

WE LEFT THE OASIS of Kanekel around two o'clock in the afternoon, for the forty mile journey back to the railhead at Guntakel. Our tickets said that three of us were booked on the 7:30 Express on Monday morning, but Shibu was booked on the midnight train to Chennai that very evening at Gooty, about ten miles up the tracks from Guntakel. Shibu was leaving ahead of us to do some family business relating to his passport status. Despite being an Indian by race, Shibu was an American by birth, as were his two children. For years he had been trying to get a dual-citizenship so that he could go in and out of India more freely. He was hoping that the meetings he would have in Chennai, Tamil Nadu would help in that quest. We would meet again just west of Chennai later on Monday for the final train-ride back to Kerala.

It took us two and a half hours to travel the field roads and dirt roads back to Guntakel. The pace was slow, but the journey was pleasant with the sights and sounds of the desert. We once again saw plenty of goats and sheep and water buffalo. In one small town we were delayed because a couple of buses blocked the road. There were the occasions when a flock of goats stopped us for a few minutes, and the pothole that would swallow us until we came up over the other side. I was told that in the rainy season there were sections of the Kanekel and Guntakel road that were impassable, and I could see why. I still recall the part of the trip where we were literally traveling in open desert up and out of Wadi after Wadi, and then on a corner as we turned around a massive thorn bush was a bullock cart loaded of brush. We had to let the cows and the cart and cordwood and their driver move on before we could; the road was that narrow. It was on such sections of the road I was warned to keep my arm inside the car or the thorns would cut my skin. Once again the heat was oppressive, but without moisture, tolerable!

We arrived back to Guntakel just before six and discovered that the motel we were going to stay at was booked solid? I wondered why, but we had to find a new motel for the night. Pasad eventually found an opening at the Paradise Motel, located on a side street just off the main artery through town. It was a modern, fancy motel and expensive by Indian standards; perhaps, the nicest boarding place in town? As we got settled into our third-floor rooms, I noticed I had filled my digital camera chip (918 pictures). I was thankful I had brought along a backup. The first thing that drew my attention was the massive cluster of bees on the ledge outside our window, and then I saw the monkeys. Taking a walk outside, I noticed a series of bee clusters under the eves. My father and I kept bees in my teens and I recognized a swarm when I saw one. The four-story motel was ideal for them, and then on the tall cell tower (yes, they are everywhere in Andrah) on the roof of the motel were scores of monkeys that used the place for safety; like the cow, a protected creature in the Hindu faith. It was then I recalled the huge Hindu temple shaped like a monkey on the outside of Guntakel, the monkey was the patron-saint of Guntakel! How sad is that?

That evening I took the gang (Shamash, Pasad, Isaac, Shibu, Shaju, and Joy) out to supper. I must admit the food at Esther's house was much better than any food I eat in any restaurant, but it was cheap. The meal of 'all-you-could eat' for seven men only cost me 600 rupees, about fifteen bucks. I put 600 rupees of gas in Shamash's car as well. We got back to the motel around eight when Shibu headed for Gooty. I remembered Solomon's exhortation:

>...and a three-fold cord is not quickly broken.
>(Ecclesiastes 4:12)

Little did I know just how important that precept would be for Shaju and Joy and I before the morning came!

53

Police Raid at Four in the Morning!

I WILL NEVER FORGET the 27th day of my 3rd Indian trip. I will forever remember the 8th day of my Andrah Pardesh adventure and the unexpected 4 AM wakeup call!

Our original plan was to sleep from ten on Sunday evening until 6:30 on Monday morning. We were less than ten minutes from the Guntakel rail station, and our train wasn't due until 7:30. After a hard week in the deserts of western Andrah, we all were looking forward to a quiet, cool (the motel had air-conditioning), and mosquito-free night's sleep. After a refreshing shower (American-like, no well water), I dropped off immediately. Joy and Shaju came in later from a setting room off the main bedroom after their showers. It seems as if I had just dozed off when a bell began to ring. Still half-asleep I thought it was the manager of the motel giving us a wake-up call. I was sleeping on the far side of the room with Joy, and Shaju was sleeping on the floor beside Joy. I got up, turned on the light by my bed and swung my feet over the side. Because my back was towards the door, I didn't at first realize what was happening. Having first looked at the clock by my bed I realized it was only four. I must admit I thought Joy was pulling one of his classic pranks. As I turned, I said:

"A bit early isn't it to catch the train?"

The words had barely gotten out of my mouth when I realized it wasn't one of Joy's jokes!

There standing in the doorway where two of the biggest police officers I had ever seen. Standing sternly in their traditional brown uniforms with a night stick under their right arms, the men had a serious look on their face, but all I could think:

"You have got to be kidding?"

I couldn't imagine what was happening, and when I saw Joy leave the room under the care of one of the officers (Joy nearly a foot shorter than the policeman), I thought:

"This can't be good?"

When you add to the fact that we all were in our underwear, they had us at a distinct disadvantage. Also standing with the officers was the manager of the motel; I recognized him from the evening before. Another handicap was they were speaking in Telugu and none of us could speak the language including Joy and Shaju. I remained on the edge of the bed with my back still slightly turned as Shaju began digging into his briefcase. A couple of minutes after he left, Joy was back with the other officer. The manager seemed to be acting as an interpreter, but at no time did the officers approach me. I sat quietly trying to be a fly on the wall as the conversation rattled on in a tongue I couldn't understand. Within ten minutes they had checked through our luggage, and as suddenly as they came, they left and we were left to wonder. They hadn't even checked my passport or visa. It appeared they were looking for something or someone, but we had and were neither.

We never did find out what they were looking for, drugs perhaps? Strangers in town, perhaps, they thought we were up to no good? We discovered later that they had raided Pasad's and Isaac's room at 3:30. Once again they came and went suddenly without giving any explanation. Sleep came hard after they left, and within an hour the local mosaic began to call the worshippers to prayer. My quiet night's sleep had turned into a nightmare. All I could think off was Russ' warning to me about this being a trip of 'firsts'; well, I had another first to add to my India list: my first police raid. Then I thought of this spiritual warning from the pen of Paul:

> Be not forgetful to entertain strangers: for thereby some have entertained angels unawares. (Hebrews 13:2)

I must admit I wasn't very entertaining to the two brown-faced, brown dressed, baton-carrying strangers that visited me at the Paradise Motel in downtown Guntakel, Andrah Pardesh!

54

Second-class on an Indian Train

AFTER THE UNEXPECTED EXCITEMENT in the wee hours of March 15, 2010, I rose to the now all too familiar sounds of an Indian city. The call to morning prayers could be heard echoing through the back alley where our motel was located. Despite the fact that most of rural India is Hindu, Islam is found in most cities, like Guntakel (our driver, Shamash, lived in Guntakel and was Moslem). I could also hear the noisy city traffic just outside the front door of the Paradise Motel as we checked out; a mixture of animal sounds and mechanical sounds and human sounds. Nobody seemed to be concerned or surprised by the early morning police raid, for it seems it is a normal occurrence in Guntakel; normal for them but a first for us, even Shaju and Joy were taken back by the event. They had traveled into Andrah Pardesh numerous times, but had never experienced such a violation of basic civil rights. Everybody in the motel staff just seemed to ignore the happening as we loaded our luggage into Shamash's car for the short ride to the train station. Pasad told us that Shibu had gotten on his train for Chennai on time, and now it was time for us to catch our train for Kerala. It was then I learned that for the first six-hours of our trip south, we would be traveling second-class!

Our train was scheduled to leave Guntakel Station at 7:45 AM on platform #6. We arrived at 7:30 to find no train, in actuality, the train scheduled before it was still in the station. By eight, the track was empty, but the platform was full. As we waited for engine #6381, I watched a huge coal train pull into the station on the other side of the platform. What caught my attention next was a trio of ravens enjoying a breakfast of discarded rice, somebody's meal just thrown onto the tracks. There is no such thing as trash cans in India; everything not wanted is discarded wherever and whenever. What fascinated me most was the way one raven open the leaf the rice was enclosed in so this buddies could share the meal, but only after he eat. As the first raven eat the other two watched; when the first raven was filled he flew over to the water fountain for a drink while the second raven eat and the third raven kept watch until the second raven was done and the third raven could eat. His feast was also watched by the two who had eaten before. Once all three had eaten and had a drink at the fountain, then and only then did they leave. I thought to myself, there is a wonderful story of sharing in the tale of the three ravens of Guntakel! Those ravens reminded me of this admonition from the pen of Paul:

> …Let each esteem other better than themselves. Look not every man on his own things, but every man also on the things of others. (Philippians 2:3–4)

Our train didn't arrive until 8:30 and it was 8:45 before we actually left the station; already an hour behind schedule, we hoped it wouldn't mess up our rendezvous with Shibu later that day? The boys of Andrah (Pasad, David, and Shamash) were there to the end as they helped us load our luggage and packages onto the second-class car. Our only moment of panic was when we realized we were on the wrong section of the platform and we had to rush through a crowd of people a 100 yards to get to our car! Joy led the way and the five of us weaved our way through the multitude trying to keep Joy in sight; sometimes a difficult thing to do because he is so short. Huffing and puffing we arrived at our door only to discover we had plenty of time because the train was taking on water.

At first, the only difference I could see between first-class and second-class was that second-class had no air-conditioning. The cars seemed to be of the same size and the compartments seemed to be just about the same. Because it was still early morning, it wasn't that hot as of yet and I must admit I really enjoyed the open windows and the fresh air blowing in as we traveled. Our final goodbyes to our Andrah friends were both verbal and visible because of the open windows of our second-class Indian train car; now, I would be able to see more clearly the coastlines along the tracks back to Kerala.

55

Indian Beggars

WITHIN A HALF AN hour we had made our first stop of the day, and it was then I discovered the biggest difference between a first-class ticket on an Indian train and a second-class ticket on an Indian train: beggars!

During the entire trip north to Andrah the week before, we had not seen one beggar on the train. There were plenty if you got off the train, but nobody harassed us, not once! The minute we pulled into Gooty Station the doors opened and a flood of individuals worked their way through our compartment. Shaju explained it to me this way. It seems that it was against the law to beggar on first-class cars, but second-class and third-class are open to anybody at anytime. Some beggars actually buy tickets on the two lower classes and ride the trains from station to station and beggar while the train is going; we would see plenty of this kind of begging during our six-hour ride in second-class. There were also those beggars who simply got on the train while the train was still setting in the station. They would get on and off before the train moved. Working their way through a compartment or two would allow them plenty of time to enter and exit.

Begging on the train came in a variety of forms. There were those that simply walked through the train with their hand out asking for money. Then there were those who had a little something they were trying to sell, worthless but at least a way for the giver to feel better. I have always had a hard time with beggars. Granted, in my lifetime I haven't been confronted with many: a few on the streets in London and Jerusalem and Washington DC. Periodically, even in Ellsworth, Maine, a beggar will come along, more often in the summer than winter: beggars seemingly don't like the cold of Maine! Yet I can say without hesitation that in six hours on the Indian train to Chennai, I encountered more beggars than all the beggars I had encountered in my entire life combined, and that includes all the beggars I had meet in my previous two trips to India!

At home I see them at traffic stops, in front of stores. In India I had see them in front of temples and at markets places, but very few have been up close and personal as they were on that train that day. In my life I can only remember a handful that have been in my face: a young man at Huston Station in London, a girl outside of the Hard Rock Café in London, a man on the Mount of Olives in Jerusalem, a mother and her daughter on a side street near New Gate in old Jerusalem, a homeless vet near a monument in Washington DC, a little girl by a Hindu temple outside Edayappara, and then there was that little girl I encountered on our way to Andrah. I was still haunted by her! Yet in a short six-hour span, every few minutes some beggar was passing by my seat in the close confinement of our compartment. My heart broke with each encounter. Shaju said, "You'll get use to it!" But I never did. It remains the most haunting time I ever spend in India. I was encouraged not to give because if I did word would spread and I would be thronged each and every time the train stopped. No man had enough money to give to them all because of the sheer numbers. As I sat watching this parade of beggars pass, one by one, I remembered the fable of the richest man in the world trying to feed all the birds in the world. He was broke before the first day of feeding was over!

The beggars on the trains came in all shapes and sizes; from adults old and tired to children with an arm or a leg missing. I was especially touched with the young man with no legs that pulled himself along the floor with his hands. Before we transferred to our first-class car, I did give money to one beggar just because we ought to try like the 'dogs' to help at least one Lazarus in our life (Luke 16:20–22). My only wish is that I could have helped the little girl on our trip into Guntakel. What good is going to a strange coast if you aren't able to help the poor and needy?

56

Hour by Hour

ON MY TRIP TO Andrah Pardesh, I had kept a trip log of the stops we made during the sunlight hours of the journey. On our trip back I decided to keep track of where we were at each hour mark. I know that many must think me silly for such record keeping, but I have always enjoyed recording while traveling. So here is what happened 'hour by hour':

1. Somewhere between Gooty and Tadpatri-boys bought breakfast for 97 rupees and two cups of coffee for 10 rupees; I still haven't seen anything worth eating! I also learned that the boys paid 7000 rupees to rent Shamash's car for the week; that works out to about $25 a day. I also learned that Shamash didn't own the car but was just the driver and he only made 1050 rupees for the week ($26.25), I was glad I gave him a 500 rupee tip!

2. Somewhere between Tadpatri and Muddanuru-Shaju sleeping, still doesn't feel good. Joy showed me a movie of a baby playing with a cobra, only in India. At the village of Kondaparum saw lots of harlots, a first for me in India. Also plenty of beggars including a one-arm man and an old lady that was bald. I was moved by a small shoeshine boy who came on the train. The air is getting warmer.

3. Somewhere between Muddanuru and Kamalapuram-I got off at Muddanruru. On the way we passed two trains, one on each side of us, so three tracks in this area. We passed again that huge power plant we saw coming into Andrah Pardesh; I still think it looks like an atomic power plant?

4. Somewhere between Kadaka and Cuddapah-stopped again to let a train pass. We are in the area of the Cuddapah stones, those flat stones they use for building. The area also has large sunflower fields. Getting warm in the car; just passed by a huge airport. Finally a peddler comes by with something I can eat: ice cream!

5. Stopped at Razampet-probably the best ice cream I have ever eaten. Strawberry, and I bought an extra tub in memory of Marnie (wherever Marnie and I have traveled together we always buy ice cream: under the Eiffel Tower in Paris or by the Pool of Siloam in Jerusalem), but I eat them both. We also stopped at a place called Vontimitta, a dusty, dirt little place, but home to somebody! We are down to five people in our eight-person compartment. I gave a blind lady 10 rupees!

6. Stopped at Mananduru-on the way we passed a huge river, a Mississippi kind of river, but it was dry except for a small trickle of water along one bank. One of our stops (Koduru) a man with a very bad skin problem (leper?); probably the most aggressive beggar on the trip. The highlight of this leg of our journey were the three bottles of 7UP we bought to share. Getting very hot, still dry, but will be nice when we finally change trains. I have enjoyed the open windows, for you are able to see the outside more clearly.

7. Somewhere between Renigunta and Tirupati-we are running nearly an hour behind. We are scheduled to change trains in Tirupati and an hour later meet up with Shibu in Kalpadi. Let us hope our second train is as late? During this hour I got off the train to stretch my legs at an unnamed station. We stopped for over half an hour to get water and for the cleaning crew to go through the train. Moved again by the beggars both on the train and off. Touch by an elderly lady that came window to window to see what she could get from the passengers. She reminded me of woman who Jesus healed from a Satanic infirmity (Luke 13:11–16).

Such were the observations I had while riding second-class on an Indian train!

57

Rendezvous at Kalpadi

A LITTLE OVER SEVEN hours after we left Guntakel, we were once again standing on a train platform with all our luggage and packages. At Guntakel we had three others to help us carry the nine pieces to the train. This time it was only the three of us to maneuver the nine articles through the maze that was Tirupati. Tirupati was a major intersection and it seemed to me that everybody was switching trains. It was a rush to find B1, but we arrived with five minutes to spare. I think Joy has missed a few trains in the past; for him the worst possible happening at any stop. I think this is why he has been such a taskmaster on this train trip. So far, I have been on time each and every time the train whistle blows; Tirupati was a flawless transfer.

At 4:30 Shaju's phone rang and it was Shibu calling to say that he was waiting for us in Kalpadi about an hour and a half away; hopefully we can pick him up before dark? It seemed that after we left Tirupati Station we stopped every five minutes. Pakala was next on our list and then Chittoor. Our compartment contained two ladies and I wondered how that would work out with sleeping arrangements as they were? Joy tried to find out if there were some open places in the car we were on, but he came back an hour later with nothing better. The best thing about the change was the air conditioning. By the time we got off at Tirupati the temperature had reached well over hundred. The car was crowded but the accommodations were comfortable compared to the alternative. I was saddened by the lady that was sitting across from me; a typical Indian wife submissive and sad!

Somewhere between Tirupati and Chittoor we changed back to an electric engine. It happened at one of the numerous stops along the way, but it was so quiet in the closed up, air-conditioned car we were in we didn't notice it until we got to Chittoor, our last stop before we picked up Shibu. I think we changed at a station called Renigunta. It was the only long stop we had during that section of the trip. Our ninth hour was spent somewhere between Chittoor and Kalpadi. We crossed the Andrah Pardesh and Tamil Nadu border at six o'clock. We stopped in Kalpadi five minutes later. Joy met Shibu at the door and brought him to our section of B1, seats 36–39. Almost immediately Shibu began to tell his adventure from Chennai to Kalpadi in a third-class car, a trip that took two hours and a half.

It seems that in third-class there are no compartments, just open cars full of seats, and, of course, no air-conditioning. In third-class anyone and anything is allowed, including animals. It is all first come first serve with no assigned seats. By the time Shibu boarded the train for Kalpadi the car he was in was full, standing room only. Almost immediately a man approached Shibu asking if he would like a seat. Was he willing to pay a few extra rupees for one? Shibu immediately said yes and a few minutes later the man returned and asked Shibu to follow him. Sure enough at the end of the car was one empty seat. Shibu gave the man thirty rupees (remember it takes about 40 to 45 rupees to equal one dollar) and sat down. It seems that there are always people willing to give up their seats on a third-class train to make a few extra rupees on their journey. Third-class is hot and smelly and crowded. People and possessions and sometimes animals are packed in like sardines. Shibu said he wanted to get up and stretch his legs a time or two but he knew if he did he would lose his seat. It was only his seat for as long as he seat in it. He was tired having gotten little sleep the night before, but his trip to Chennai was successful. He had waited 90 minutes for us at Kalpadi (this is where he got me my double order of onion rings).

We were thankful again that our Divine Travel Agent had worked out all the details, and that the steps of a good man are ordered of the Lord (Psalms 37:23) even on a third-class train in India!

58

Picking Rice out of the Dirt

As the boys eat there supper and I got into my second bag of onion rings, I began to reminisce on the whirl-wind week that had just passed me by. It seemed such a blur as darkness settled around the train that was taking me through Tamil Nadu and by morning back to my beloved Kerala. Flashes of events in Andrah Pardesh became my focus as I started to daydream and relive in my mind those special glimpses in time that only happen when you are tired.

My first remembrance was of three deer crossing our path as we travelled from Guntakel to Kanekel. The wide open spaces seemed so vast compared to the small Indian deer. The afternoon was hot and seemingly unforgiving. There was no water or grass within sight and I wondered just how they could survive in that desolate, barren land. My companions told me that I was witnessing a rare sight in the desert of central India. My first thought came from the psalmist when he wrote:

> As the hart (deer) panteth after the water brooks,
> so panteth my soul after thee, O God. My soul thirsteth for God, for the living God: when shall I come and appear before God? (Psalms 42:1–2)

These three deer were searching for food and water as they jumped across our path that Tuesday afternoon, I wonder if I was as driven to seek the water of life (John 4:14) and the bread of life (John 6:48) in my daily wanderings?

My second memory was of a little girl as she herded five water buffalo through a back alley of Kanekel. She seemed so small in comparison to the huge animals walking before her. She had a stick in her hand, and periodically, when one or another of the beasts stopped moving she would slap them on their back. I was moved by her dirt complexion and tattered dress and the very idea that someone so small, and a girl at that, was doing such a disgusting job. I was on my way to David's house for lunch, and I wondered if the little lady would get lunch? No doubt, she was directing these five water buffalo to water or grazing, but what of her? It was then Jesus' admonish to "suffer little children, and forbid them not, to come unto" (Matthew 19:14) Him that struck my soul like a thunderbolt. I wanted to reach her for Christ, get her out of this terrible lifestyle, but how?

My third recollection that evening on the train heading south was of a lady beside the road as we neared one of the rural churches we traveled to for afternoon services. We often saw people beside the roadway doing something. There were road crews fixing damage done during the rainy season. There were laborers working in the countless fields scattered beside the dirt roads we travelled. One image remains to this day. As we slowly maneuver around a deep pothole, we came to a section of the road were the local people had put their cut rice bundles out to dry. They also would put the straw in the road so the traffic would beat the rice from the stacks. I had never seen anything like it, but what caught my attention wasn't the strange method of extracting the grains of rice. There on the side of the road was a middle age lady setting, but what was she doing?

By the time we got parallel to her the sun was beating down on her in its full fury. It was unbearably hot, and the dust kicked up by our tires was a choking cloud that engulfed her as we passed. She never moved from her task that now I could clearly see. She was picking rice out of the dust, one grain at a time! Her head down and with no reaction that she had even seen us pass; she was focused on the bits of foods she could gather from the dirt they had fallen into. In all my years, I had never seen anything like it, nor had I imagined that there were people in the world so poor, so short of food, that they would spend a hot day setting in the dirt beside a rural road to salvage small, dirty grains of rice. When Jesus said, "For the poor always ye have with you . . ." (John 12:8), I never imagined I would ever see such poverty. As with the beggars on the train, my heart was grieved over the fact that there was nothing that I could do to change her estate. They were in the care of God, and God alone, and I had to be content with that!

59

Night Train to Kochi

HERE ARE MY JOURNAL entries for our travels from Tamil Nadu to Kerala:

We rolled into Jolarpettai Station around seven thirty. The platform was dark, the darkest on the trip. We stopped long enough for me to buy the boys a bottle of water (24 rupees for three big bottles-less than twenty cents apiece). Shibu has just gotten off the phone with Pasad. He had called to see how we were doing. The people in our compartment don't seem to be as eager to go to bed as did the group we traveled north with. I am tired and now that the Discovery Channel (the longer I stayed on the trains in India, the more they reminded me of the documentaries I had watched on television at home about traveling in foreign places) is no longer being broadcasted through the train window, I am ready for bed!

My first three hours in the middle bunk contained little sleep. My companions were night hawks. There were the lights, the talking, and of course, lots of cell phone calls to listen too, even if I couldn't understand the languages being used. I tried to block it all out, but my mind just wouldn't settle down. At least I was lying down, a bit of rest I guess! Right around eleven, the car seemed to settle down, and I did drop off to sleep, but a steady, deep sleep was hard to come by. I tossed and turned trying to find a comfortable spot on the seat cushion, but there was none to be found. I was warm enough with the light blanket they provided, but my long legs and wide body was no match for the surface area provided for my sleep. I must have slipped into some kind of undisturbed slumber near four in the morning because I never heard the train stop to let Shibu off in Kochi.

I was a bit disappointed that I wasn't awake to say goodbye to Shibu. Waiting for him at Kochi Station was our faithful driver Binu with Shibu's car. The boys told me that it was around four in the morning when our train pulled into Kochi Station. On my very first trip to India I had flown into Kochi (Cochin), Kerala's most cosmopolitan city. It is the main trading center in the state and it was built around a saltwater lagoon off the Arabian Sea. The city itself is actually just a collection of narrow islands and peninsulas jutting out into the water. I had only spent a few hours in Kochi, but because it was my first taste of India it has become a special place for me. I hadn't been back, except for this early morning stop, and I slept through it! Sad!

Shibu had gotten off in order to attend the graduation of a small Bible college just north of town. The school's president, Pastor Sam, had attended Kerala Baptist Bible College's graduation and Shibu wanted to return the favor. I am continually amazed by the obligations afforded in India. Respect and honor is given to each individual and it is seen as honoring to pay your respects for such visits. Shibu had already been 41 hours on the road since we left Kanekel, and because of this side trip he would be another twelve hours before his trip was over. We on the other hand will be back to Edayappara in just a few hours!

The boys had me up by 5:30. They didn't want me to miss getting off the train at Kottayam. If I slept through the stop they would have to pick me up in Trivandrum, 100 miles to the south. Because the stops are often quick, we were standing in the doorway with all our stuff and Shibu's stuff as the train entered Kottayam Station. Lulu was waiting for us with the staff car, exactly 22 hours after we left Guntakel. My first Indian railroad trip was over, but was it my last? It is my desire to take at least one more train trip through India to visit again my friends in Andrah Pardesh, and to hopeful travel on to Orissa. I also have a former student from KBBC that now labors for the Lord in the State of Chhattisgarh in a region called Bastar; he has invited me to come and visit him and I can think of nothing better than to travel to see him on Indian's infamous railway system, I enjoyed my trip that well, despite the agony I experienced with the poor beggars of India! Paul once again came to mind this morning when he wrote to the Church of the Thessalonians:

> In everything give thanks: for this is the will of God
> in Christ Jesus concerning you. (I Thessalonians 5:18)

And I was thankful for the journey and the companions I traveled with. Despite the fact it was shorter than my Australian experiences, it was by far the greatest spiritual adventure I have ever taken to date! I know the Lord will 'enlarge my coast' even further afield if He should tarry!

60

Saying Goodbye to Anna

I GOT BACK TO the Simon house just about an hour after I had gotten off the train in Kottayam. It was pure joy to take a shower with warm water. It was even better to take a three-hour nap in a big bed. I slept like a baby until two in the afternoon. Despite the increase in humidity and the 120 degree temperature, the fresh water, comfortable bed, and ceiling fan made everything 'a-ok' for me. I got up and sorted a little and packed a little for my trip home; just a day and a half away. By three Shaju, Julie, and Jerry had picked me up for a final run into Kottayam to pick up a few things for home: Indian tea for my wife, cashews for me, and a few presents for some special friends. We also were going to have supper together in a fancy Kottayam restaurant, a kind-of-going-away party. I also wanted to say goodbye to someone that had been a part of very trip I had made to India!

My love of the Indian elephant has only grown since my travels to its native land. I have studied the warrior's use of the elephant since the days of Alexander the Great and Hannibal. Then to actually see the Indian elephant in the wild and to actual get on the back of one during my first trip seemed enough, but then on my second trip I had gotten to ride an elephant and actually play with a number of them at an elephant reserve. Periodically, I saw elephants as I traveled around (four so far on this trip which takes my personal sighting over thirty), but there was one elephant I had seen on each of my trips to Kottayam, but I had never stopped to say hello. I was determined that on this last day in Kottayam, I would stop and say goodbye to 'anna' (Malayalam for elephant).

Enlarge My Coast

This special 'anna' was a lumberyard working elephant that lived under a massive teak tree just inside the city limits of Kottayam. I still remember the first time I saw this big male from afar. Located on one of the main roads into Kottayam, you have to pass the lumberyard if you're coming in from Edayappara. My first glimpse was just that, a sudden sighting of the biggest elephant I had seen up until that time. Its blackness (because of the shade of the tree it was under) and its huge white tusks revealed only part of its size. I was determined to get up close and personal with this elephant before I headed back home on Wednesday. As Shaju drove us into town, I asked if he might stop for a few minutes by the lumberyard so that I might get a close up photograph of the elephant; he was agreeable, if I promised not to get to close; he knows me to well, I still have no fear of the massive creature called elephant!

Sure enough, as we pulled off the road across the street from the lumberyard, 'anna' was standing in his usual spot swaying in the late afternoon breeze. I quickly got out of the car and carefully made my way across the busy street (a very dangerous adventure). I had to climb over a number of large teak logs ready for cutting in order to get close to 'anna'. Instead of a forklift, the elephant is still the primary mover of logs in India's lumberyards and forestland. The time for sawing lumber seemed to be over for everything was still in the yard as I worked my way toward the calm creature. There were a couple of men near the elephant eating, so I asked if I might get a picture, to which they didn't seem to care; they ignored my request and presence. I got as close as I dared, and it was then I noticed the elephant wasn't even shackled. The only thing keeping him in place was a tall, thick pole against his trunk (it was only later I learned that elephants are taught to hold onto something and as long as that something is touching their trunks they will not move until the object is removed). It was such an amazing thing to see that elephant totally under control with such a ploy. It reminded me how Satan often keeps people in place with such simple things, when in reality they are free to walk away at any moment, but like the elephant in Kottayam are trapped by Satan's training! (II Corinthians 2:11 and II Timothy 2:26)

61

Strawberry Ice Cream

AFTER A FEW PARTING moments with my elephant friend at the Kottayam Lumberyard, Shaju took me to a small appliance shop to pick up a stone mortar and petal for my daughter Marnie. On Marnie's last trip to Kerala she had brought one for herself, but because of the weight wasn't able to return to the States with it. I decided to surprise her with one. The hand-carved set only cost me 95 rupees ($2.25). After a few more purchases, we went to a small restaurant for supper; a farewell meal with my good friends, Julie, Shaju, and Jerry. I had a cheese sandwich and French fries; yes, you can find American food in India if you try (the Simon's did have something Indian). We top the meal off with strawberry ice cream, and Jerry had two scoops, how that boy loves his ice cream! I chose strawberry in remembrance of my experience on the train, and I must admit the ice cream on the train was better, maybe, it was where I was and what I was going through that added to the favor. The restaurant was air-conditioned and the surrounding very pleasant; unlike the time I eat the strawberry ice cream on the train. Our trip into Kottayam ended as all trips to Kottayam did with a stop at the G-Mart, India's version of Wal-Mart. My last purchases were pepper, tea, and cashews!

We got back to Edayappara just in time for my 'farewell' service. There is a tradition in the IGBC that each and every guest gets not only a welcome service but a farewell service as well. About fifty of my Indian friends came out to say their final goodbyes and to pray for my safe trip back to America. Shibu, Shaju, and I sang "To God Be The Glory" again to the delight of the people. Both the boys (they have become more like sons than co-workers) spoke and KJ Thomas had the closing prayer and Pastor George, the new pastor of the Kangazha Church, lead the meeting. As with my other farewell services, I felt like I was leaving family and friends, not strangers. The service lasted about an hour and there were plenty of handshakes and hugs to end it all. Most of the orphans were there and the mission staff. My month ministering with them had been some of the best days I had ever spent in the service of the King of Kings. I was reminded of these instructions from the pen of Paul:

> And we beseech you, brethren, to know them which labour among you ... and to esteem them very highly in love for their work's sake. And be at peace among yourselves. (I Thessalonians (5:12–13)

Smooth as ice cream.

I ended my last day in Edayappara trying to call Dallas, but got only my daughter's answering machine. However, about an hour later I got a call from Dallas and had a wonderful talk with my wife and daughter. It was time to reconnect with my American family as I said goodbye to my Indian family. It was all starting to sink in that another wonderful "India Journey" was coming to a close. I climbed the staircase in Shibu's new home for the last time and was in bed by ten. It had been a long day that started earlier that morning on a train from Andrah Pardesh, and now here I was in my upper room, my prophet's chamber in the Shibu home. Sleep came quickly as I settled into a satisfying rest; I knew that tomorrow would be another long day as I started the marathon trek that would eventually get me back to the coast of Maine. As with my other two trips to India, I was leaving India with no regrets and only fond remembrances of the time I spent with some of the best people I have ever had the joy of ministering with and too. I slept in the sweet melody of the psalmist that wrote:

> Behold, how good and how pleasant it is
> for brethren to dwell together in unity! (Psalms 133:1)

United, unified, and a unit is how best to describe the people of Kerala. We would do well to aspire after such accord in our assemblies. Like the sweet taste of strawberry ice cream on a hot and humid summer day on the coast of India!

62

Last Day in Edayappara

I SLEPT LIKE A baby, a full ten-hours, before I woke to a terrible head cold and some troubling mouth cankers. I had felt them both coming on for days, but ignored them as I enjoyed my final hours in India. One of the blessings of God to me is "…for so He giveth His beloved sleep." (Psalms 127:2) Despite physical hardships, I have always been able to rest and I give my Lord all the credit. He knew that I would get no rest on this my last day in Edayappara. Before the day was through I would start the 36-hour journey back home. My dear wife would also be travelling today from Dallas (where she had spent a week with our daughter) back to our home on the coast of Maine. So how would I spend my last day in my home away from home?

I had my last breakfast with the Simon kids (Joshua and Abigail) just before they were off to school. It was a wonderful interlude that started our days in Edayappara together. I am not an oatmeal kind of guy, but in India it tastes good as Jos would say with plenty of sugar! After breakfast I was off for a final walk-about town. I was hoping the hot, humid weather would start clearing out my plugged sinuses. I decided to walk from Shibu's to Mary's house (John's widow); I wanted to deliver a sympathy card with some money. On the way I wanted to take a few more pictures of the town just in case this was my last trip to this beloved Indian village. I wanted some photographs lest my mind fade in the future. I never want to forget the place God used to teach me of the importance of native mission works and just how sweet brothers and sisters of a foreign land can be.

It took me over an hour to make the walk, and by the time I got back to the Shibu house my sinuses were a bit clearer. Waiting for me was my dear friend Joy Thomas and his wife. Shibu had driven them over for a final goodbye. We exchanged gifts (a very Kerala thing to do) and had a departing prayer. My prayer for him was that he would be able within a short time to move back to Orissa. His prayer for me was that the day would come that he would be able to show me Orissa himself; we are still praying for that day to come (in 2012 that prayer was answered, an adventure I will share in my next India book-The Uttermost Part). I have claimed this verse from Acts 15:36 as Paul said to Barnabas:

> "Let us go again and visit our brethren in every city where we have preached the word of the Lord, and see how they do."

My last meal in Edayappara was at Shaju's house where Julie fixed me baked potatoes and fried chicken, and for dessert, strawberry ice cream! After lunch I walked over to the mission office to say farewell to the staff. I climbed again to the top of the five story structure to see how the work on the fifth floor was progressing. I had watched the fourth floor going up in 2006 and it was nice to see the final floor project near completion. The walk back to Shibu's was hard and by the time I reached the home the outdoor thermometer in front flower garden read 124 degrees. Despite the heat, I was pleasantly surprised to find a 5x7 photograph of the new Venmony sanctuary and parsonage waiting for me. While I was away Pastor Regi had come by with the keepsake. He wanted me to see the church without the tent blocking the front of the structure. That picture sets on a shelf behind my church desk, a continual reminder of a vision fully realized!

By late afternoon, I was up from a two hour power nap. I started the last of my packing, always a difficult process because of the last minute gifts from these generous saints. By eight I was taking a final shower and putting on clean cloths. By ten the boys had gathered (Shaju, Binu) and by ten-thirty we were on the road to Trivandrum Airport.

63

Reviewing the Trip

BECAUSE OF THE IMPROVEMENT in the roadway from Edayappara to Trivandrum, I was dropped off at the airport at 1:45 AM on March 18, 2010, three hours before my departure flight. It took me less than an hour to get through customs and immigration and security. With time on my hands, I decided to review what happened on this third trip to India. My journal needed to be updated in a few areas as well. So now I share with you some interesting discoveries as I waited for Qatar Flight #241 out of India.

The first thing I noticed was that I had visited or revisited 13 of the churches and mission outreach works of the IGBC. It was a pleasure to meet some of the new pastors who had taken pastorates since my last trip; men like George of Kangazha, Robin of Mukkada, Binu of Koch Kamakshi, Sawgee of Thopramkudy, and Lawrence of Vanniyoor. It was also nice to meet again some of the old pastors that I had gotten to know on my previous two trips; men like Thomas of Poovanmala, Thomas of Edairikkapuzha, Joseph of Vrindamvanam, Ranjan of Ranni, Regi of Venmony, Paul of Kachani, and Sachi of Ooruthambalam and Narnai. From Edayappara, I had travelled over 600 miles to visit these sister churches of Kangazha.

The second thing I noticed was that I had the privilege of preaching 49 times in my month in India, 27 times in Kerala and 22 times in Andrah Pardesh. Included in those messages were my first funeral service, my second graduation message, and third farewell sermon. Besides the speaking engagements, I also gave away ten of my books (I now have had four books published through Wipf and Stock Publishers out of Eugene, Oregon) to former students, members of the IGBC staff, and the Simon family. Also included in the these opportunities to speak were the fulfillment of these desires I had before I arrived in India: the desire to see and speak at the latest IGBC church plant at 58 Colony, the desire to go to and preach at the only two IGBC churches I hadn't preached at in Narnai and Ooruthambalam, and to preach the dedication service at the new Venmony sanctuary!

The third thing I noticed was that I ultimately got to visit and meet pastors from five different states in India (Kerala, Orissa, Tamil Nadu, Andrah Pardesh, and Karnataka) and learn more of 44 pastorates (21 during my stay in Kerala and 23 in my stay in Andrah Pardesh). It was such a joy to revisit old friends, like the boys from Orissa, and to make new pastor friends, like the boys from Andrah Pardesh. You have probably noticed that I have used the word 'boys' numerous times in this book whether talking about Shibu and Shaju, or many other pastors. The reason I have done this is that they are mostly younger than me. I would say that 95% of the pastors I met in India are all younger than I am. Only a handful will live into their 60's. I have become the 'elder' to many of them, and that is why I feel that I have gotten such respect from these men, men who have certainly done more for the Church of God than I could even imagine.

The final thing that caught my attention as I waited my flight out of India was the 98,942 ($2247.13) rupees I was able to give away on this trip. When I ended my 2007 trip to India the Lord directed me to this verse in Deuteronomy 14:28:

> "At the end of three years thou shalt bring forth all the tithe of thine increase the same year, and shalt lay it up within thy gate."

What the Lord said to me through that verse was to set aside funds for my next trip to India. My tithes I give to my local church, but the Good Lord so increased my ability to also give an offering to India. This doesn't include the $5000 my wife and I gave to finish the Venmony project. We can ask the incredible and do the impossible when God is on our side (Luke 1:37), even on a foreign coast.

64

Blessings and More Blessings

As I waited my four-thirty morning departure from Trivandrum Airport, I flipped through my "Enlarge My Coast" journal. I had been making 'lists' of things that happened on the trip as well as a day by day accounting of my journey through India. I have always been a 'list' person. I have my daily list of things to do, and on a trip like I was on I liked to record certain things; like the sermons I preached, the places I visited, the miles to those destinations, and a list I called "Great Spiritual Blessings" based on Ephesians 1:3:

> Blessed be the God and Father of our Lord Jesus Christ, who hath blessed us with all spiritual blessings in heavenly places in Christ.

You know by now that I think India is a 'heavenly place'!
Here are some of the things I recorded under this heading:

1. Visit to Tamil Nadu to see the 24-year ministry of Pastor Lawrence in Vanniyoor and the 50-year ministry of his father in Tholady.
2. To see Russ Coffin's face as he present a new red-scooter to Pastor Paul, the fulfillment of Russ' desire to help the pastors of Kerala.
3. The joy of handing our awards at Bethany School to over 300 students for academic and sports achievements.
4. To see the unity and fellowship of the staff at KBBC in their annual cookout at Shibu's house, the fellowship was sweet even if the food wasn't!
5. To be given the honor of unlocking the front-door at the new Venmony

Baptist Church for the first time, and being the first to enter the new sanctuary.

6. To have Russ with me on the first two weeks of the trip, and to see his face and to listen to his voice as he experienced for the first time the mystic of India.
7. Traveling to Andrah Pardesh with Shaju and Shibu and Joy on Indian's ancient railroad system through the hills of Kerala and Tamil Nadu.
8. Seeing 22 people get saved in my first 5 services in Andrah Pardesh was a spirit altering experience for me!
9. Meeting again my friends from Orissa in Kanekel and to hear their incredible stories of survival through the persecution of 2008.
10. To be the keynote speaker for the Andrah Pardesh Annual Convention and to see 15 hands raised at the invitation and to see 11 come forward for salvation.
11. To play apart in the ordination of five men into the churches of Andrah and to be one of 715 who came to witnesses their ordination.
12. That despite the four AM raid of the Guntakel police, we got in and out of Andrah Pardesh without any major problems.
13. Ultimately saw 54 people make professions of faith in our six-days of meetings in the churches of Andrah Pardesh.
14. To hear from my friends at the Kangazha Church that after my final farewell service that if I come again I will not be welcomed as a visitor but one of them!
15. That I had time to prepare 37 sermons inspired by India to be shared with my people at Emmanuel upon my return.
16. That I had time to write 64 hymns and choruses based on old tunes and music I have been singing for a lifetime.
17. That I was able to see to the completion of a vision I had in 2006 for a new church structure in Venmony, India in 2010.

You can never do anything for the Lord that will not be ultimately rewarded by Him in the form of some kind of 'coastal' blessing!

65

Daily Record

ANOTHER INTERESTING PAGE IN the back of my trip journal dealt with the daily hours, weather, and study time I spent between February 17, 2010 and March 18, 2010. These columns helped me keep track of my days in India. This is what I recorded daily:

Date	Hours in Day	Weather	What I Prepared
2/17/10	14	on the plane	3 sermons
2/18/10	13 ½	on the plane	1 sermon
2/19/10	19 ½	hot/humid 100+	2 sermons
2/20/10	18	hot/humid 100+	2 sermons
2/21/10	16 ½	hot/humid 100+	3 sermons
2/22/10	16	hot/humid 118	1 sermon

(According to the national weather report the hottest place in India today was Kerala; all temperatures are based on Shibu's thermometer in the front flower garden of his home.)

Date	Hours in Day	Weather	What I Prepared
2/23/10	14 ½	hot/humid 116	3 sermons
2/24/10	17 ½	hot/humid 115	2 sermons
2/25/10	16	hot/humid 122	1 sermons/1 song
2/26/10	15 ½	hot/humid 120	1 sermon/4 choruses

(One of the rare days I have spent in India, for it rained a little today only third time in nearly seventy days in India I have actually seen it rain, if but a shower.)

Enlarge My Coast

2/27/10	16 ½	hot/humid 119	1 sermon
2/28/10	15	hot/humid 118	1 sermon
3/1/10	16	hot/humid 110	4 CHORUSES

(Today I saw the slowest temperature on Shibu's thermometer, and that was at 75!)

| 3/3/10 | 15 | hot/humid 117 | 2 sermons/ 8 choruses |
| 3/3/10 | 18 | in the mountains | 2 sermons/4 choruses |

(In the 10,000 foot mountains the weather is cool and mild compared to the foothills. This was my 3rd day into the mountainous country of Kerala and by far the best weather.)

| 3/4/10 | 15 | hot/humid 116 | 3 sermons/ 4 choruses |
| 3/5/10 | 14 ½ | hot/humid 115 | 3 sermons/10 choruses |

(A rare night had a lot of thunder and lightning tonight, but very little rain with it!)

3/6/10	15	hot/humid 114	3 sermons/8 choruses
3/7/10	15	hot/humid 120	2 sermons/5 choruses
3/8/10	16 ½	on the train	NOTHING
3/9/10	23	hot/dry 100+	3 songs
3/10/10	16	hot/dry 100+	1 sermon/1 song
3/11/10	16	hot/dry 100+	4 choruses
3/12/10	16	dry/windy 100+	3 sermons/10 choruses
3/13/10	16 ½	cooler/cloudy 90+	3 sermons/10 choruses
3/14/10	15	cooler/cloudy 90+	3 sermons/10 choruses

Daily Record

3/15/10	20	on the train	3 sermons/10 choruses
3/16/10	22	hot/humid 120	3 sermons/10 choruses
3/17/10	16	hot/humid 124	3 sermons/8 choruses
3/18/10	34 ½	on the plane	NOTHING

(Remember, I gained back the 10 ½ hours I lost on my way to India!)
 The Psalmist once exhorted:

> So teach us to number our days, that we may apply our hearts unto wisdom.
> (Psalms 90:12)

I can honestly say I have never spent more productive or meaningful days than the days I have spent on the coasts of India!

Postlude

Returning to my Coast

ON MARCH 18, 2010, my flight out of India began at 4:30 AM. It would be another long day, 34 ½ hours before I arrived back in my native Maine. Five minutes into the flight the pilot announced that it would take us 4 hours and 10 minutes to make Doha, Qatar 2037 miles away; that the weather was perfect and we would be cruising at 32,000 feet over the Arabian Sea and flying at 537 miles per hour. As I settled into my first flight of the day, I added up just how many miles I had already traveled on this journey "from coast to coast".

On the way to India I travelled by car from my home on the coast of Maine to the Bangor International Airport 32 miles away. I boarded a plane from Bangor to JFK Airport in New York adding another 417 miles to my trip. From New York it was on to Doha, Qatar a flight of 6697 miles, and then on to Trivandrum, India 2037 miles away. So by the time I arrived in India I had already covered 9183 miles. During my stay in India I kept track of just how far it was from place to place. Just in Kerala I made 24 trip to various churches and places before I even headed to Andrah Pardesh and these trips covered another 740 miles, all by car. My first train ride in India covered 671 miles from Kottayam to Guntakel, and then it was back in a car. I took 15 trips in Andrah Pardesh by car (I will never forget the two miles I travelled between Garudachedu and Thumbiganoor by bullock cart!) which covered another 215 miles before we retraced our steps back to Kerala. All told I travelled 2503 miles in India, and another 18,302 miles to come to India and to get back to my coast. Before my day would be over I would finish my trip at 20,805 miles!

Each time I take such a trip I am reminded of the wonderful gracious hand of the Lord that covers me and protects me. In this day of terrorists and accidents, it is a relief to know that you have someone going ahead and clearing the way. This is exactly what I felt happening as I made Doha, Qatar right on time. I had about an hour and a half layover at Doha International Airport. Russ and I had come into Qatar in the dark, but it was early morning and I got to see a few sights. The airport is about three miles from downtown, and the reputation of this Arab State was all I had read. It was a cool 78 degrees and the cloudless sky allowed you to see far beyond the airport. I was impressed with the richness I saw, but it was soon time to board Qatar Flight #83 for New York and to find seat 11C for the 13 ½ hour flight to the east coast of America.

My flight home to the USA took me over Europe and Greenland and eventually down across Eastern Canada into New York City, how many coast would I have seen if we had been flying low enough to see? I watched three movies and got a catnap or two as the day drug on and my sinus got worst and worst. A headache came about halfway through the flight, but a couple of aspirin seemed to fit the bill and I was able to tolerate the final few hours. We eventually landed around three in the afternoon. It took me about an hour to get through customs and immigration and find Gate 25 for my flight back to Maine. That flight was on time, and my wife was waiting for me at Bangor, and in actually time, from Edayappara to Ellsworth, it took me only 32 hours to cover the 9283 miles between these two distant coasts. This is another marvel of the age we live in when those before us would take days, weeks, and months to travel between shorelines and I did it all in just a day and not even a half! I have always claimed this promise for such trips:

> For He shall give His angels charge over thee, to keep thee in all thy ways.
> They shall bear thee up in their hands, lest thou dash thy foot against a stone.
> (Psa. 91:11–12)

Now you know way I have no fear of travel, whether auto or air, boat or bullock cart! And why it is a blessed opportunity when the Good Lord in His wise providence 'enlarges your coast'!

www.ingramcontent.com/pod-product-compliance
Lightning Source LLC
Chambersburg PA
CBHW050827160426
43192CB00010B/1920